FUNNY YOU SHOULD ASK:
HOW TO SELF PUBLISH
A BOOK

GETTING YOUR BOOK OUT THERE ON
AMAZON AND BEYOND

LORI CULWELL

GW00778419

LEGAL NOTICE

GET FREE UPDATES!

Before we get started, I want to get you set up with a way to get future updates for this book. The industry of self-publishing is dynamic and constantly evolving. As such, I make frequent updates to this guide and re-publish it at least once a quarter so all of the information is the most current it can be.

Why am I telling you this?

Here's the thing– *I* want to provide you with the most updated version of this book (whenever there is a new one) and am happy to give it to you for free, but once you buy the book, I have no way to send you the update. Contrary to popular belief, Amazon (or whatever other platform you bought this book on) is not going to automatically push out the most updated version of the book to people who have already bought it. That kind of sucks, and I'm trying to change that, one book at a time.

So, here's my request: please go over to https://loriculwell. com/htsp and sign up for updates. Whenever I put out a new version of this book, I will immediately notify you that it's time to download your updated copy of the eBook version. To further incentivize you, I will also give you a free copy of the companion guide I created for this book!

If you bought the eBook version originally, great! You'll simply download the updated version and move on.

If you bought the paperback, also great!! You'll get a free eBook version with free updates to go along with it

So, come on over to https://loriculwell.com/htsp. There is a ton of information coming out about self-publishing all the time, and I don't want you to miss out!

CONTENTS

1

WHAT IS GOING ON HERE? WHO AM I? AND OTHER QUESTIONS

Welcome! You're reading this because a) you wrote a book and want to self-publish it, b) you read something else I wrote, found me mildly amusing, and want to know what else I can teach you, or c) you bought this book by mistake. It happens!

Whatever the reason, I'm glad you're here! I am one of those people that believes that everyone has a story to tell, and if I can help you through the process of self-publishing while also making you laugh a little along the way, I will have fulfilled my purpose in life.

So, hi! I'm Lori. A little about me: I have been a writer for most of my life, having published in places like the Huffington Post, Entrepreneur, and salon.com, as well as in several actual magazines and even print newspapers (old school!). I've also written a bunch of books and have experienced every publishing method out there, from traditional publishing to "hybrid" publishing to straight-up self-publishing. I'm going to let you guess which one I like best. :)

Actually, here's a fun fact about me (maybe it's my claim to fame?): I am one of the few authors that can say they wrote a novel, self-published it, marketed it myself, and sold so many copies, Simon & Schuster bought it and re-released it.

Oh, that happened, and it involved MySpace, if you can believe it. If you want to read that story, you can find the 30-second version of it here: https://loriculwell.com/story

Since then, I've written many other books, tried many more marketing methods, and have helped with books and book marketing for authors, agents, and publishing companies. Through all of that, I have developed a good system for putting a book out there yourself and making it successful—and I am excited to share that with you now!

It's a lot of information (compiled over a lot of years of trial and error, some of which involved crying), but I'm going to try to make it fun. Or, at least as fun as this stuff can be. I'm told I have a knack for taking what can be seriously dry subject matter and making it more palatable with a bit of humor here and there. A reader once called my style "snarky, yet informative," which sounds about right.

. . .

Who is this guide for? What are you going to learn here?

This book is for you if you have written a book (or you have a book in your head, or you're almost done with a book) and you've decided you're going to self-publish it. I'm so excited for you because self-publishing is now more accepted by the mainstream world than ever before, and while I don't think I would call the process easy, it is definitely doable. I am here to walk you through all the steps to self-publishing, from formatting your book to researching its keywords to choosing the right trim size to understanding the rather tricky upload process for ebooks, paperbacks, and hardcovers. I'll help you decide whether you need to buy your own ISBN (and I'll explain what that is), whether to print your book in color or black and white, and how to choose the ideal category for your book so it really stands out. I cover everything in great detail so you can go through the process confidently and come out the other side with a book you're proud to share with your friends, family, and fans. I even cover how to get some fans!

The guide is organized into three sections: Part one outlines all the stuff you'll need to do before you go to upload your book into the KDP system. Part two walks you through the upload itself (again, just so, so many moving parts), and part three details the launch and the follow-up. This is where I show you how to get your book some wider distribution, how to set up reporting, and even how to run some paid advertising, if you choose to do that. Part three also touches briefly on author platforms and marketing. Not too much, though! This is not even the book for that!

How does it work? How difficult is this going to be?

· · ·

So....done correctly, the self-publishing process from beginning to end is actually more difficult than Amazon makes it sound, especially if you do all of the things a traditional publisher would do, including the marketing bits. I'm here to reassure you that all of it is very doable—though I do hear a lot from first-time self-publishers that the whole process was more of a "journey" than they expected. That's actually the very reason I put this book together! I want everyone to be able to do this! And really, maybe I'll over-explain things to the point where you'll laugh at me when you actually get in there to upload, because you'll find that it was easier than I made it sound. It would be great if you were that over-prepared, wouldn't it?

Also, I based the extreme thoroughness of this guide on the presupposition that you are coming to the self-publishing process with absolutely no knowledge. If you've already done all (or even part) of this before, it will be so easy!

What will I find in this guide?

I like to learn something and then take immediate action, so that's how I structure my instructional guides. Throughout this book, I will feed you information in bite-size pieces, and then I will (usually very strongly) recommend that you go and do the thing I just told you about.

You'll have to trust me on this. Doing it this way will not only make you feel great about your progress, but it'll also ensure that everything sinks in along the way. You're going to hear me ranting—

often in all caps—about how important these little steps are to the whole process. But here's my promise to you. When we get to the middle of this book and you're ready to plug in all the various components necessary to get that book of yours published and pushed out in the world, you're going to thank me. (Oh, yes. You will thank me.) But more importantly, you are going to thank YOURSELF.

Might as well get used to the all-caps thing now.

Can I publish my book for free?

Yes, you can! Publishing your book on Amazon is free, and you can do all of the steps I outline in this book for free, or by asking your friends or trading with someone who has the skills you need. Your ultimate goal is to get your book out there in the highest quality form it can be right now so you can take the profits and reinvest them back into your business (your current book, future books, author platform, etc). I'm going to make several recommendations in each section for both free and paid options and you can decide from there what you want to pay for. Ultimately, you'll want to make the best book you can with the budget you have and bootstrap from there!

Your Crossroads Moment

At some point along the way (ok, it's Chapter 7), you are going to need to decide if you are just putting your book out for yourself or if you're doing it because you actually want to sell some copies and start making money as an author. This choice will determine how you approach the work, how you feel about your results, and, ultimately, how you define success. It will be a crossroads moment for you!

Maybe you already know. You don't have to decide right this minute, but you will have to decide when we get to Chapter 7. Don't worry. I'll remind you of this moment.

What If I Get Overwhelmed and Want to Quit?

Listen, I'm not going to lie—this book has A LOT of information in it. Just take it step by step, and you'll totally get there!

To help you work through all of it, I have created a companion guide/workbook where I have boiled this whole book down to something like 40 pages, plus I've given you a bunch of space to take notes. You'll get a free copy of that when you sign up for the electronic version (and the updates) over at https://loriculwell. com/htsp

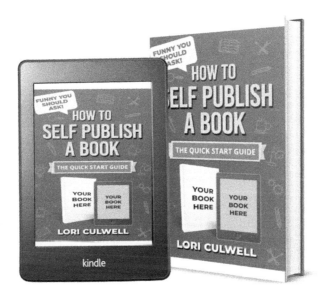

Okay, time to get started. I hope you're excited! Let's use this momentum to jump right in and get you organized and set up for success!

Let's go!

PART 1: PREP

If you've read any of my other books, you'll know that the first step in my process is always to have you prepare all the things you'll need to get through this thing I'm trying to teach you before you actually start doing the thing. From years and years of working with clients on their books (and writing/publishing books of my own), I have compiled a thorough list of the things you're going to need before you hit the "log in to KDP to upload my book" phase.

Here's why we're doing this: it has been my experience that one of the main frustrations of self-published authors (that I have heard about, anyway) is that they log in to KDP before they are really ready, get overwhelmed by the list of requirements, and crap out before that book is actually published. That, or they panic and make bad decisions that are supposed to be temporary (like publishing their book without keywords) just to finish the publication process, and then never go back to fix those temporary decisions and ultimately get upset because their book isn't performing better.

I don't want this to be you, so I am going to give you an exhaustive list of stuff you need to do and gather before you even log in and start trying to put your book into the KDP system.

I'm serious! If you go through this entire list and get everything ready, your self-publishing process will be amazingly smooth, and you will send me joyful messages when you become a bestseller.

Before you upload your book, you'll need to:

1. Perform a thorough analysis of your book's competition

2. Finalize your manuscript, get it copy-edited and proofread

3. Decide on the actual size your book is going to be (trim size)

4. Format your manuscript properly for that size

5. Get a cover designed or design it yourself

6. Research keywords for your book

7. Research the Amazon "Browse Categories" your book will go in

8. Write your book description

9. Make sure your "author marketing bare minimum" is in order (yes, I'm serious)

10. Learn meditation

I'm sort of kidding about that last one, but sort of not. The self-publishing process requires some (okay, a lot!) of patience and deep breathing, especially the first time through. I believe in you, though! You can do this!

During this first section, you are going to repeatedly wonder why I am making you go into such detail before we ever log in to upload your book. I hope that you'll put your faith in this process and put the prep work in, though, because once you get to the upload process, it's going to make sense and be totally smooth sailing. For real! This is what people tell me!

For organizational purposes, you'll need a couple of folders on your desktop (or a set of documents in Google Docs/Sheets/whatever) where you'll keep everything publishing-related. I would recommend (at least) the following:

(Book Title) interiors: this is where you'll keep in-progress versions of your manuscript and the finalized version. You'll need to refer to your completed interior file(s) when you communicate with your designer, plus you'll need to know exactly where to find your interior at several points in the upload process. Take the time now to establish where you're going to put those files so you don't waste time hunting for them (or, God forbid, upload an old version and end up printing that. Nightmare!).

(Book Title) research: this is where you'll keep things like your competitive analysis, keyword research, category research, and so on.

(Book Title) covers: this is where you will keep all the versions of your book cover, including eBook, paperback, and hardcover. This just in: they are all different sizes!

(Book Title) marketing: hopefully you'll already have a main "your author platform" folder going with the logins for all the elements of your author platform (website, email list, socials, etc.) If you don't have an "Author Platform" folder, definitely make one of those now. This marketing folder is book-specific and is for things like keyword research for future advertising buys, ideas for articles/press releases, and so on.

That's it! Look over the list of "things to do" so you know what you're in for, make those folders, and you're good to go!

2

THIS IS AWKWARD

This is one of those moments that goes without saying, but here I am, saying it anyway: I am assuming that if you are reading this book, you are largely finished with your manuscript.

Let's talk about what I mean by finished:

1. You are done with the actual writing of your book (seems self-explanatory, but you'd be surprised)
2. Someone (not you) has copy-edited your book
3. Someone (a whole different person, also not you) has proof-read your book

Optional (but recommended):

. . .

4. Someone (a person who will tell you the truth, i.e., not your mom) has read your book just to make sure it's what your market would determine as "good."

Let's be clear: I'm not telling you what to write, nor am I saying that I am the arbiter of what's good. That is not for me to say (like, at all). And by "good," I don't mean "is the story good?" or "is the (non-fiction) material good?" I don't actually care about that because you (ideally) know your market, you know what your audience wants, and you know what is already selling. I have stopped giving my opinion about the kinds of books that I think will sell because almost every time I say something like "That's a terrible concept for a book," that book becomes a bestseller, and I'm sick of being wrong. Listen: go ahead and publish your paranormal romance series about wombat people from the planet Azcabam or your comprehensive guide to eating only green food. Who am I to tell you what you feel like writing?

That was a weird sidebar, but trust me when I say I have heard some really odd pitches for books.

"Good" in this context simply means finished—like the story is done (or, for non-fiction, the book says everything you set out to say when you had the idea), and copy-edited and proofread; like it's not full of egregious errors that will take away from the story or material.

If you do not do this, here's what will happen: someone is going to buy that book and read it, be bothered (offended, even!) by the errors, and leave you a one-star review on Amazon. This is going to really hurt, because:

a) that person will not be wrong. Again, books are a business, so if you're selling something, it should be market quality. You should have taken the time to make sure your product (i.e., your book) was the highest quality possible before you put it out, and;

b) errors take away from the overall thing you are trying to do with the book, so you should definitely spend the money on a copy-editor and proofreader to make sure things like typos and grammatical errors don't derail your efforts. I'm serious!

Here are some places to find editors and proofreaders:

1. Ask your friends and colleagues. This is my first go-to method, and it usually works. If someone you know is an author, ask them whom they used as their copy editor and proofreader and if they had a good experience with them. You can also barter for this if you are trying to do the whole process for free. I promise you that at least one of your friends is an obsessive proofreader.

2. Upwork: https://www.upwork.com/hire/copy-editors/ . I have hired several excellent professionals on Upwork.

3. Reedsy: https://reedsy.com/

. . .

4. Fiverr: https://fiverr.com/ (try to stick to "Top-Rated" sellers with a lot of reviews)

5. BookBaby: https://www.bookbaby.com/book-editing-services/

One note about these services: you'll want stand-alone services like copyediting, proofreading, and cover design, *not* an all-inclusive package that includes the actual publishing of the book. The publishing is what we are covering here, and I want to make sure you don't lose control of that process (or overpay for something I am about to teach you). Just get the services from these places (if you choose to), and then come back to this book when your manuscript is finalized.

Here's another potential "gotcha" moment (especially for bloggers): Before you publish your book, you're going to need to go through and remove any work that is going to appear in your book from anywhere else it currently appears on the internet. Amazon's terms of service prohibit you from publishing work that is "freely available," which means if you are publishing a book of essays that are on your author website, you will need to remove them, then give the internet a month or two to forget about them before you publish your book. Amazon does, in fact, scour the internet to make sure your work is original, and if they catch you duplicating work (*even your own work*), that is going to be a problem, and they are going to send you a scary email. If you have that issue, make sure to solve it before you publish. You've been warned!

. . .

Just so you know, this chapter has been relatively short, but that's not because I somehow naïvely believe these things don't take a long time. Finishing your book alone can take years, people!

What you don't want is to be almost done with formatting, only to decide that your book could really use another chapter (or two). That's going to throw your timeline off and increase production costs, so my best advice is to work and re-work the manuscript until you are totally confident and you don't even really see the words anymore, *then* start this process.

If you're good, I'm good, so let's start by turning our attention to the main competitors for your book.

3

THE COMPETITIVE ANALYSIS

Okay, you are organized and mentally prepared to do some prep work, so we are jumping right in on the research portion of the self-publishing program. First, we're going to take your book idea to Amazon and get a feel for what your competition is doing over there.

Here's what we're doing: back in the olden days of traditional publishing, before you wrote your actual book, you'd write a book proposal (for non-fiction books at least). The proposal would include a full breakdown of the table of contents, a little summary of what each chapter was going to be about, a section on your target demographic and the intended audience, a section on marketing ideas, and then the all-important "Competitive Analysis" section. This is where you would name and describe the most successful books already on the market in your subject area (your competition), and then make the argument as to how your book would differ from those popular books.

. . .

This is one of the things I have carried over from the old-school publishing process, and I'm really glad I learned it because it's saved me a ton of time and hassle over the years. I am still very much in favor of doing this exercise when self-publishing, so I will walk you through doing just that right here, right now.

It should be no problem for you to find some competitors for your book, especially if you're a big fan of your topic or genre. You've probably even read a few of these books, or you've at least seen them floating around in your peripheral vision as a reader, and you probably also have a good idea of your peers/other people who are writing books in this genre or category.

If you have no idea what I'm talking about or where to start with this, just go over to Amazon and type in some general keywords you think would get you to a book like yours and see what comes up. For example, if you've written a book about meditation, type in "meditation books."

When I did that, here are some of the results I got:

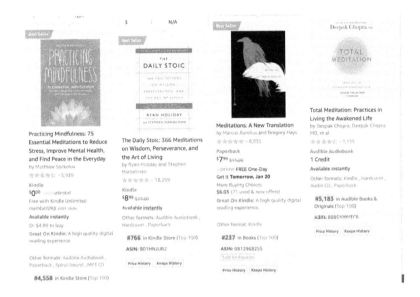

To do a competitive analysis of this (or any) theme, you would just click into each one of these books and start writing down all the particulars about them.

You're going to be taking a bunch of notes for each title, so I would start a new file on your computer for them because you're going to be referring to this throughout the entire process of self-publishing. Put it in the "(Book Title) research/marketing" folder you just created.

Here's everything you'll need to write down for each of the 5-10 most popular books on this subject:

· · ·

1. What is the average **physical size and page length** of the most popular books on this subject? Are most of them 6 x 9, 150 pages? I'm just throwing those numbers out there because that is probably the most popular size and length of books on Amazon, but you'll need to do some research into your topic and genre and see for yourself. Make notes of the size/page length of the top 5-10 bestselling books you think your book will be competing against.

2. What is the average **price** of the top 5-10 books on this subject? You'll want to price your book to be competitive with the others. Too low and you'll make people wonder about the quality of the book, too high and you'll price yourself out of the market. You think this doesn't matter, but it's one of the first things I look at when troubleshooting a book that's not selling. Often times I will find that the price of the book in question is wildly out of sync with the rest of the books in that segment.

3. What do the **covers** of these 5-10 books look like? Take a screenshot of each and put them in the folder. You will be sharing these with your designer (or referring to them if you are designing the cover yourself). You're trying to get a feel for the dominant themes of the genre and give your designer (or yourself) some inspiration when it comes time to make the cover. I'm not saying you should copy anyone's cover! Don't think I'm saying that! Don't write to me and say I said that!

4. How many **reviews** does each book have? This will let you know how difficult it might be to start being competitive against those books.

. . .

5. Speaking of reviews, go through and read your competitors' one-star reviews. Try to figure out what people don't like about these books, and make darn sure that your book doesn't have any of those problems. Did that author leave something out? If so, add that to your book. Does that author's manuscript have typos or formatting errors? I know you'll do this anyway, but make sure you have a great copyeditor in place to make sure that doesn't happen. Every one-star review against a competitor is your own goldmine of insight into "what not to do."

6. What **Amazon Browse Categories** is each book ranking for? Do not even worry if you don't know what browse categories are right now, because we're going to cover that topic at great length in a bit. Click into each book's listing and scroll down until you get to the "Sales Rank" section (which looks like this):

Best Sellers Rank: #148,031 in Books (See Top 100 in Books)
#362 in Personal Time Management
#33,775 in Religion & Spirituality (Books)

You'll need to pick three categories when you upload your book into Amazon's KDP system, and now is a good time to start thinking about what you might want those to be. If you don't do this, there is a risk you might choke and put your book into the vast wasteland of a category known as "Uncategorized," where it will never be seen or heard from again. Authors that put their book into the "Uncategorized" category often cry, and I don't want you to cry.

. . .

7. Keyword research—what **keywords** is each book ranking for in Amazon? Did you know you can easily do a reverse-analysis of books on Amazon to see what they are ranking for? I am going to start yelling (okay, writing emphatically) soon about how important keywords are to the health of your book and how you can NEVER, EVER LEAVE THE KEYWORD SLOTS BLANK (uh-oh, it's happening already), so start jotting down some keywords that represent what your book is about. Is it non-fiction? Philosophy? Self-help? How-to? You have to start somewhere with this, and now is the time. This is one of those exercises that seems stupid and unnecessarily time-consuming when you're doing it, but later you're going to be absolutely thrilled that you have this information because many of your competitors are not going to do this.

8. Links—while you're making this list, go ahead and copy the link to each book's listing on Amazon, then paste it into your research document. You'll need to refer back to each book later when you start writing the description/summary of your book.

In case you were super into this or the other exercises and want some extra-credit material, I would highly recommend checking out Publisher Rocket (www.publisherrocket.com), which is a paid software that lets you do even more in-depth analysis into everything from the average page length of the top-ranking books for any given keyword to income predictions for your competitors' books. Every bit of information you can gather at this stage helps!

Great job! I'm sure your mind is positively overflowing with information and new ideas, so take a moment to organize your notes and screenshots. In the next chapter, we're jumping right into keyword research!

4
KEYWORD RESEARCH! FUN!

Because I have a background in search engine optimization (SEO) and marketing, I believe that authors should be doing keyword research *before* they even start writing their books.

When I say this to authors (especially authors of fiction), some of them will roll their eyes at me like I am some kind of cold-blooded marketing weirdo. They don't want to do research! They want to be free, to write what they want to write!

I am also an author myself, so let me just say for the record that if you have a book in your soul and it just really needs to come out, *let it out*, friend! I'm really not trying to tell you what to write; I just want you to do keyword research so you can position yourself to actually sell some copies of your masterpiece when it comes out.

. . .

Here's the deal: Amazon is a marketplace where you can buy books (and just about everything else), but it's also a powerful search engine, and ignoring this will cost you money. If you've ever gone to Amazon and searched for a particular keyword (which is how most of us find everything, right?), you'll know that Amazon is masterful at showing you the perfect thing for that keyword because they want you to stay in their world and buy their stuff.

Simply put, keywords indicate **demand**, and books (or products) are the **supply**. You go to Amazon and type in "intermittent fasting for weight loss," and bam! Amazon will show you all the latest and greatest books, audiobooks, journals, and whatever else they have to fulfill that need. They are *not* going to let you walk away empty-handed.

Here's how this applies to you: as an author, you need to tell Amazon what keywords your book should appear for, so they can use your book to fulfill that need when people type in those keywords. You do that by putting keywords into your metadata (your title, subtitle, and the seven keyword slots you were asked to fill in when you published your book, if you put it out yourself). Amazon will then "index" your book for those keywords, meaning it will start matching and associating those keywords with your book and showing that book to people who type in those words.

I'm emphasizing the keyword thing so much now because, frankly, the upload process can be overwhelming for first-time self-publishers, and I have found that the keyword boxes (arguably one of the most important parts of Amazon's discovery process for your book) often get skipped or filled in haphazardly because the author just wants to see their book in print, and/or just wants the process to be over.

As an author, I get it. But as a marketer, that kind of thing keeps me up at night because those empty keyword boxes represent so million missed opportunities for your book.

Also, I have found that it doesn't matter what kind of book you've written—*everyone* needs to fill in those keyword slots. Whether you've written a paranormal teen romance or a fix-it book about boats, Amazon still needs some words in those slots to figure out when to show your book.

Okay! I have now convinced you that you need some keywords. So, where do you go to find them? If you are already familiar with the keyword research process (because you make websites or some-thing like that) and have a go-to software that you like, feel free to use that. If you don't have a preference, I'm going to show you a few different ways to compile a list of keywords. Full disclosure: I use Publisher Rocket (an excellent paid software) and the paid version of another great software called Helium10 for this, but you can totally get some good keywords using just the free version.

You can also just go right on over to Amazon, type in your main keyword, see what autocomplete keywords Amazon shows you, and write those down. That looks like this:

I have the free "AMZ Suggestion Expander" plugin installed, which you can find over at: https://loriculwell.com/amzsuggest

Any keywords are better than none, but I would rather have you just do the research right the first time so that you have some great stuff to put in those keyword boxes. I think you'll be pleasantly surprised by what this exercise produces—and it'll give you the confidence to move forward in the whole process. Trust me. Once you get to the upload section, you're going to be really happy you did this.

Just to make sure you've covered your book's keywords from every conceivable angle, here is an "old school" list of questions for generating some keywords (which you can also use when you are writing your book's description and summary in Chapter 6). Just go through and answer all of these questions (use a pencil and paper if you want!), then save the answers to use when you're filling out the keyword boxes during the upload.

. . .

1. What kind of book is it? This is the "high level" question again. For fiction, you can use words like "fiction, series, paranormal, mystery," or whatever genre you're publishing in. For non-fiction, I would include the words "non-fiction," then drill down. Is it a book of essays? Is it a self-help book? Cookbook? Say something describing something! You'll also want to use words indicating what kind of book this is, like "paperback, Kindle eBook, hardcover," and so on, and I always throw in the word "book" for good measure because I am a nerd. Believe it or not, people still search for books using the word "book"!

2. What does your book have in it? This is your chance to describe the content of the book in keyword form. For our "paranormal teen fiction" example, we would put those words, then "vampire, werewolf, gnome, princess," and whatever other characters you might find in that book. For non-fiction, I would describe techniques, topics, tools, and anything else you cover. Did you write the definitive encyclopedia of cheese? Now is your chance to list all of the cheeses.

3. Who is most likely to read this book? This is a question for determining your target audience. Who did you write this book for? Your list might look like this: women, teens, moms, romance lovers, girls, men, grandmas, etc. At first, all authors say "I want everyone to read my book," but eventually, we realize that not everyone's going to like what we're dishing out, so give this one some thought.

4. Why might someone buy this book? This is an "occasion" or context question. Your list might include: birthday gift, Christmas, education, textbook, self-help, and so on.

. . .

5. What does it seem like your competitors' books are optimized for? You can usually tell if a book is optimized for keywords by looking at its subtitle.

Those were the "manual" methods of pulling keywords, and they will work just fine for a first-time publisher. If you're in a super competitive genre or you want to go much deeper into your keyword research, I have two paid suggestions for you. The first one is Helium10.

If you followed my "competitive analysis" instructions, you'll hopefully have a list of 5-10 books that you would consider your main competition. Your first and best move is to see what keywords those books are ranking for.

First, go over and sign up for a "starter" account at www.Helium10.com. This account is $29/ month and you can stop it or start it anytime you want, so most authors I know will turn it on for a month when they are about to launch a new book. Helium10 is an excellent research and analysis tool that is mostly used by people who sell physical products on Amazon, but it works great for books and publishing.

Once you've signed up, you're looking for a feature called "Cerebro," which is a nifty reverse search that will let you spy on your competitors' keywords.

To do your keyword research with Cerebro, you'll need to grab the ASIN of each book on your competitors' list. You can find that on each book's listing by scrolling down until you see this:

Product details

ASIN : B0779RF557

Publisher : Coffee Break Publishing (February 1, 2018)

Publication date : February 1, 2018

Language : English

File size : 1901 KB

Simultaneous device usage : Unlimited

Text-to-Speech : Enabled

Screen Reader : Supported

Enhanced typesetting : Enabled

X-Ray : Enabled

Word Wise : Enabled

Print length : 266 pages

Lending : Enabled

Best Sellers Rank: #6,737 in Kindle Store (See Top 100 in Kindle Store)
  #18 in Metaphysical Fiction

  #50 in Contemporary Fantasy Fiction

  #89 in Women's Fantasy Fiction

Customer Reviews: ★★★★☆ ⌄   1,356 ratings

Click "Cerebro Reverse Product Lookup" in Helium10 and you'll see this screen:

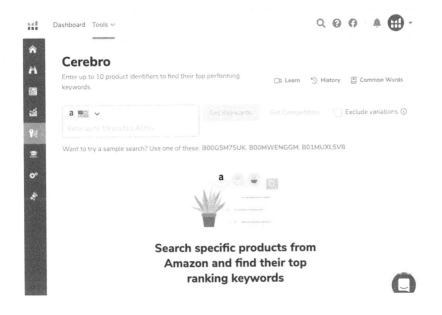

Take the ASIN of the first competitor and put it in the space. For this example, I am doing a reverse search on my own book, "Funny You Should Ask: How to Make a Website" (which, yes, you should totally read if you want to know how to make a website).

As you can see, my book is ranking for 369 keywords, which means that Amazon knows what the book is about and is serving it up when people type those keywords into the Amazon search box. Cool!

· · ·

I obviously didn't put 269 keywords into the seven keyword slots (not because I didn't want to, but because there isn't enough room for that), so that means Amazon has taken the information I have given it about my book, combined that with real people's search and buying habits, and is adding keywords of its own.

If I scroll down a little bit, I can actually see all 369 of these keywords. Here is a screenshot of that. I have blocked out the keywords because, a) I don't want to give away too much of Helium10's secret sauce, and b) those are my own book's keywords. Come on!

As you can see, Helium10 gives you a bunch of information for each keyword, like search volume, competing products, and the "Cerebro IQ score." You're not going to be able to sort these columns and really dig into this information with a free account, but just having this list will help you build an overall keyword set for your book. The good news is, if you've even gotten this far and done this step, you're way ahead of probably 90% of self-published authors with books out there.

. . .

Please note (important!): this is one confusing moment that can trip you up later, so I'm going to take the time to explain it here. Some of the keywords you find during these searches are going to be the names of other authors and their books. It is NOT OK for you to use those words as your keywords. It is okay for AMAZON to rank your book for these keywords, but it is NOT OK for you to intentionally put these keywords in your metadata.

For example, my book IS ranking for the term "newsletter ninja," which is great for me because I love Tammi Lebreque's books and I do think our audiences overlap, but *I did not put that title in my back-end keywords*, nor do I ever mention it anywhere in my book. Amazon has determined, on its own, that when customers type in "newsletter ninja," it might also be good to offer them my book (yay!). I did not use that title anywhere in my keywords because that would be a violation of Amazon's Terms of Service, which I do not do under any circumstances.

Sorry for the semi-ranty sidebar, but I wanted to make that clear. You're just looking for the general keywords and key phrases for which Amazon is ranking your competitors' books, with the specific purpose of being able to use those words as your keywords. I would never, ever try to get you to do sneaky things that violated Amazon's Terms of Service. You wrote a great book! You don't need to be sneaky!

You'll need to repeat the reverse-search process for however many books you have in your "competitive titles" list, which should give you a decent list of 25-30 keywords. If you're sticking with the free Helium10 account, that's going to take you a few days (or maybe a week) because you can only do two searches per day. You could also subscribe for a month, do all of the search stuff you need to do, and then unsubscribe, but I am trying to give you the cheapest option for every single thing first. If this is the method you're using, put those keywords into an Excel Spreadsheet or Google Sheet, save them in your "Research" folder, and you're done! Feel free to move on to the next chapter.

If the Helium10 method doesn't appeal to you, another way to do keyword research for your books is to use Publisher Rocket, which you can get at www.publisherrocket.com. Publisher Rocket is amazing, and I love it, and you will use it for many publishing-related things, but no pressure! I want you to be able to bootstrap your very first book with little to no cost!

To use Rocket to pull your keywords, you would need to have a general keyword or phrase in mind to start (because you can't do that reverse-search on people's keywords with this software).

I started with "website" and got this:

Keyword	Average Pages	Number Of Competitors	Average Price	Average Monthly Earnings	Est. Amazon Searches/Month	Competitive Score	
	246	>1,200	$ 17	$ 2,164	<150	79	
	285	>1,200	$ 17	$ 128	>100	26	
	364	>1,200	$ 20	$ 2,260	>100	28	
	328	486	$ 16	$ 2,103	>100	25	
	466	>1,200	$ 22	$ 5,405	341	43	
	411	>1,200	$ 22	$ 4,610	357	40	
	115	>1,200	$ 7	$ 657	>100	60	
	103	>1,200	$ 8	$ 79	<100	20	
	211	>1,200	$ 13	$ 62	>100	49	
	580	>1,200	$ 23	$ 406	<100	20	
	203	83	$ 25	$ 18	<100	30	
	438	>1,200	$ 25	$ 4,402	<100	40	

I have blocked out the actual keywords generated by this software out of respect for the developers of Publisher Rocket since it's a paid product, but I did just want to show you how many keywords and key phrases are generated just by starting with the word "website."

This is your place to quickly build a solid keyword list for your book, plus it shows you which words and phrases are competitive, how much search traffic those words and phrases get, and how much the top-ranked books for those keywords are earning. This information is all great to know for your current book, and it'll probably give you some ideas for other books you can write!

For this method, you would keep doing new searches like this within Publisher Rocket until you have a list of 20-25 keywords/key phrases that are related to your book.

Just some quick side notes and dos and don'ts regarding keywords here, and then I will let you go and do one (or all!) of these exercises to compile a keyword list for your book:

DO a reverse-keyword search on every book in your competitive analysis to see what keywords that book is ranking for. For this, you just need the ASIN for each book (which should be in your competitive analysis spreadsheet), and you can use the "starter" version of Helium10 (www.helium10.com).

. . .

DO keep a spreadsheet of words you used, so you can repurpose that research for your description and your book marketing.

DO NOT repeat words. This is not only a waste of that precious keyword space, but it is spammy and annoying to Amazon (if robotic algorithms can be annoyed). Some experts will disagree with me as to whether repeating words actually hurts, but I like to stay on the better-safe-than-sorry side of that kind of thing. The minute they decide they don't want it and start searching for people who are doing it, you're at risk of that being an issue.

DO NOT use competitor names, copyrighted terms, or words that don't actually describe your book. This violates Amazon's Terms of Service and can get your account shut down. Your paranormal teen fiction novel probably *would* be a great read for people who loved Twilight, but this is not the place for the words "Twilight" or "Stephenie Meyer." You'll want to keep a list of words like that to use in a paid advertising campaign, because that is where you can actually use those types of words and phrases.

I use all of these methods for my books and clients' books, and I find using one or more of them usually yields enough keywords to not only fill in the keyword slots in the back-end of KDP, but also to use in marketing materials, emails about the books, and social media.

Great job! You've got your keyword list done, and now we're moving on to researching categories!

5
CATEGORY RESEARCH

O nce you've got a thorough list of all the keywords for which you want Amazon to rank your book, it's time to move on to researching all the categories where you'll want it to appear.

Category research is another one of those "hidden gem" areas that you'll *definitely* want to do before you start actually uploading your book. If you don't do this research beforehand, you are very likely to end up panicking and haphazardly sticking your book into a terrible no-person's-land category like "Non- Classifiable."

DO NOT BANISH YOUR BOOK TO NON-CLASSIFIABLE LAND! Categories are a huge and often-overlooked opportunity!

Whoa! Sorry! I started yelling again. I cannot handle it when people rush through choosing their categories. Second only to your book's keywords, categories are a super important part of your book's discoverability within the Amazon system. Also, there is also a cool thing you can do with categories to make your book a bestseller, so please do not underestimate the value of good category research at this stage in the game!

You're probably wondering: can your category choices really help you sell books? Are Amazon's categories really that different than the traditional BISAC categories from the publishing world? If that's true, why aren't all authors doing this?

The answers are: yes, very, and I don't know.

Categories are a whole world within Amazon, and surprise! That world is keyword-based. Because they love to do everything their own way, Amazon has invented their own categorization system called "Browse Categories" with over 16,000 different little subcategories (as opposed to the approximately 4,000 BISAC categories of the traditional publishing industry). Amazon is a data-driven company and they are constantly testing and tweaking this system to help them sell more stuff, so you might as well use it to your book's advantage.

To see what I mean, pull out your competitive analysis again (when will I stop mentioning that pesky exercise? The answer is never!) and take a look at some of the categories that your favorite books are ranking in.

· · ·

Just as a reminder, books are displayed within Amazon by their BSR (best sellers rank) by category, which looks like this:

Best Sellers Rank: #517,299 in Books (See Top 100 in Books)
   #626 in Paganism
   #1,059 in New Age Mysticism (Books)

This example book is ranking #626 in the "Paganism" category. The top level of the bestsellers' category for Paganism looks like this (note that we are four levels down in Amazon's hierarchal Browse Categories system at this point):

After looking at the best seller ranks/categories of just a few titles, you'll start to notice that no book is in just one category (like Non-Fiction > Social Sciences). On the contrary, Amazon puts each book into multiple tiny categories and sub-categories, and they are showing you three categories at a time for each book. This system is designed exactly like the link hierarchies of old-school SEO, driving targeted traffic down to the "inner page" that is your book's listing.

On the surface, this category system looks like something that is just happening on the back-end and seems like it wouldn't really impact you as an author, but I will prove to you that with proper research, you'll be able to find a category so small, your book can be its # 1 seller.

And really, isn't that why we all started writing in the first place? So we could call ourselves "bestselling authors"?

I'm kidding. Sort of. That's not *why* we do it, but it sure is nice when it happens!

What you need to accomplish this neat trick is to dig into the depths of all the categories and sub-categories that are relevant to your book until you find one that has a #1 bestseller (for that category or sub-category) that you know you can beat.

Why?

Because when you put your book into this category and then get enough people buying the book to beat the current #1 seller, Amazon will give you one of these cool little badges:

. . .

Funny You Should Ask: How to Make a
Website: The 100% Not Boring Guide to
Setting Up Your Website with Wordpress
Kindle Edition

by Lori Culwell - (Author)   Format: Kindle Edition

Book 1 of 1: Funny You Should Ask

#1 New Release   in Internet Culture

See all formats and editions

Kindle	Paperback
$4.99	$7.99 / prime
Read with Our Free App	1 New from $7.99

Who needs a website these days? Let's see— are you a human person existing in the

Did you think I was bluffing about this technique?

OH NO NO! I have tested this extensively on my own books (and books I have worked on for clients). That screenshot (and many others), are in fact, framed and hanging up on the wall of my office. I teach by living the experiences, people!

Since I'm assuming I now have your full attention and you are super motivated to do this research, let's jump right in!

Category Research: the Manual Method

First, I will outline how to do this research manually. I want to give you the lowest-cost way to do everything because I want you to save as much money as possible (especially on your first time through the self-publishing gauntlet), so when I say "manually," please be aware that I do mean "free" and "time-consuming." If you want to see the way to do this with *paid* software, please skip to the section called "The Paid Method."

Starting with the "Books" link in the Category sidebar, click on every category and sub-category that is remotely relevant to the topic of your book. Put these categories into a spreadsheet. Be sure to also include the BSR (best sellers rank) of the book that is #1 in that category.

You will probably find that some of the categories overlap with keywords/key phrases you found in the last exercise, and that is a great sign that you're on the right track. If you've never paid a lot of attention to categories and sub-categories, you are probably going to be shocked at just how hilariously granular Amazon gets with its categorization system.

As you can probably imagine, each sub-category has fewer books in it than the one above it, making it easier and easier to become a bestseller the further down you go.

Write down each category and sub-category you might want your book to go into, then click down into each to see the best-selling books. Next, take the BSR of the top books in each category and sub-category and run those through this excellent (and free) little tool (https://kindlepreneur.com/amazon-kdp-sales-rank-calcula tor/) to determine how many books per day those books are sell-ing. That way, you'll know how many books per day *you'll* have to sell to get that orange badge. Put those numbers in the spreadsheet.

In case that was too much theoretical information flying at you at once and you are now overwhelmed, here's a real-life example:

One of my recent clients had a book that launched in the "Political and Social Sciences" genre, and I did this exact research for him as part of helping him publish his book. The initial temptation would have been to just stick that book into the Books>Politics & Social

Sciences category, but that would have been a waste of an opportunity to put that book into smaller, less competitive categories where it could earn one or more bestseller badges.

For this example, I started by looking through his book's potential categories one by one, then looking at the bestseller ranks of the top-selling books in each category. In the "Journalism Writing Reference" category, for instance, the #1 seller has an overall sales rank of 2,158. To achieve that BSR, he would need to sell 59 books in one day.

That was probably going to be a little too ambitious (based on the size and conversion rate of his email list), so I kept looking around until I found the "Public Affairs" category, which looks like this:

In case you're thinking, "Hey, my Amazon search results don't look like that! Are you a wizard?" No, I am not. The individual bestseller ranks are displayed all on the top page courtesy of a nifty, free plugin for Chrome called DS Amazon Quickview, which you can find here: https://chrome.google.com/webstore/detail/ds-amazon-quick-view/jkompbllimaoekaogchhkmkdogpkhojg?hl=en

As you can see, the book that is ranked #1 for this category has an overall sales rank (meaning, in all of Books) of 30,124.

When I take that number and run it through the Sales Rank Calculator, I get this:

What this means is that to achieve #1 status in this category, this book is selling 7 books per day.

Obviously, the other (more backward) way to approach this is to determine how many books you think *you* can sell (based on your email list, social media profiles, paid advertising, etc.), then look around until you find a category where you can be #1 with that amount of sales. Same difference, sort of, but the first one leads with the content, the second with the numbers. That was a boring insight that you probably did not need, but here we are.

What you'll need to do is keep poking around until you find ten categories that a) only need an amount of sales you think you can actually generate to get to the #1 slot, and b) are relevant to your book's content. I know, ten sounds like a lot, but once you're in the groove, it's pretty easy to spot them, and you're going to need these categories at several upcoming points in the self-publishing process, so take the time and get all of the research out of the way now. You'll thank yourself several chapters from now!

I know I just dropped a lot on you, but before I move on—I know what you're thinking, and we should talk about it before we go any further.

You're, like, "Um... that was really complicated and seems like it could take hours, and I do not have the time for that."

Understood. There is a (much) faster way to conduct this research and come up with these successful categories, but it does involve a paid tool, so I wanted to just give you the manual, free way to do it so you wouldn't feel like I was dangling some secret method in front of you that you could only get by paying. I am not that person!

The Paid Method

The faster way to do this process is to pay for some cool software to sift through all the categories for you and tell you where to put your book so that it can hit #1. This software is called Publisher Rocket and was created by a self-publishing and marketing genius named Dave Chesson. I think you should invest in it without delay, and if you know me at all, you know that I am not the kind of person who ever wants you to pay for something if I don't use it myself. Hell, I am the person who wrote a whole book about how you can make a website for $25 and gave you every money-saving strategy I had along the way. I am totally serious about saving people money, so when I not only buy something myself but also endorse it, you know it has to be something.

Here's how Publisher Rocket solves the "which category should I pick?" problem. You type in a word, and Publisher Rocket searches all of the categories, giving you an estimate of how many books you would need to sell to get to the #1 slot:

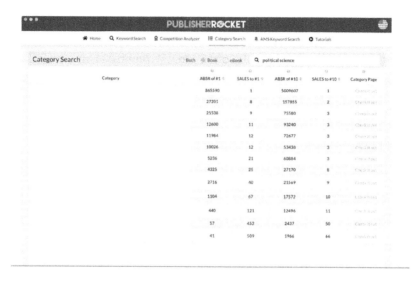

I have blurred out the categories Publisher Rocket came up with because that is their proprietary technology and I want to respect them.

I will say that Publisher Rocket is the one tool I think you absolutely cannot live without as a self-publisher, for this as well as many other reasons. Publisher Rocket can also give you a list of keywords for you to put into the keyword slots, tell you what words to advertise against, and do your competitive analysis for you.

My final plug for Publisher Rocket is that I think you can gain a competitive edge in many areas of self-publishing for a relatively small investment by using it, which is going to really help you because many people who self-publish want to get everything for free. (I said what I said)

. . .

A word of warning: DO NOT, and I mean DO NOT UNDER ANY CIRCUMSTANCES, intentionally put your book into a category where it doesn't belong to try to game the system and get a good ranking in that category. That is not what we are doing here at all. That is a blatant violation of Amazon's Terms of Service and is grounds for terminating your account.

I'm going to say this in a nice way, without actually name-checking anyone: If you have recently watched a YouTube video about intentionally putting your books into the wrong categories in order to drive more sales, that advice could not be more wrong, and you should not do that. I'm not sure how much longer that person's channel is going to be up, but do not listen to that advice.

Was that subtle enough? Probably not. Go ahead and message me if you want to know the channel I'm talking about.

That's it for now!

6

YOUR BOOK'S SUMMARY, BLURB, AND DESCRIPTION

Okay, you've done your competitive analysis, made your keyword list, and found your ideal categories. While all of that information is still fresh in your mind, let's take that energy and use it to write your book's summary, blurb, and description. You might have already written one or more of these things (as part of a book proposal if you did one, as an outline, or just in your notes about what your book was going to be about before you actually wrote it), so this should be pretty easy to pull together. Besides, you wrote the damn book, so you know what it's about, am I right?

Summary, blurb, and description (oh my!). What is the difference between these things, and why do I continue to make this process so difficult for you? When am I going to tell you how to put your book into Amazon already?

. . .

Hang in there. This is another one of those things that is definitely going to make more sense later in the book, but you have to stop and do it sometime, so I've decided that time is now. I figured you just did some analysis and research, so now was as good a time as any to sit down and write some stuff *about* your book.

So—summary, blurb, and description. The main difference is length, but also tone, as well as where you'll actually be using each one. It'll also be great to have some stuff written about your book when you get to the marketing part of the process.

The **summary** is just the one-to-two line explanation of what the book is about. The **blurb** is what you put on the back cover or book jacket to sell it (and what you would tell someone if they said, "Oh, you wrote a book? Cool! What's it about?" That one should be about 250 words (or more if you have the space and are feeling loquacious) and should also include a little author bio. The **description** is what will go in your book's listing on Amazon, also to sell the book. They allow you 4,000 characters for that one, which is about 650-1000 words, depending on the length of the words you choose.

Let's break each of these down.

Summary

You probably already have some version of your book's summary in your mind, but if you don't, now's the time to write that down! Right now, write a sentence or two that encapsulates the highest-level thing your book is about. This is the "what" of your book.

"My book is about: _____."

Great! Now you have your summary down on paper (or computer) and can begin expanding from there.

Blurb

Next, you need something for your designer to put on the back cover of your printed book (and for you to include in press releases), so we're going to expand your summary into a paragraph that describes not only the high-level thing your book is about but also includes a little more detail about what the book covers, as well as some biographical information about yourself as an author. All of this should convince someone to buy the book.

If your book is fiction, you'll want to describe the circumstances of the main character's journey. Fiction readers are looking for entertainment and escape, so tell them something about your book that will hook them in!

If your book is non-fiction, you'll want to discuss some of the ways you solve whatever problem the reader has. Now would be a good time to get out your keyword research to give you some insights.

You'll also want to include some authority-building language in your author bio, just about why you are qualified to write that particular book. You also might want to include some quotes from people who have read the book and loved it, if you happen to already have some of those.

Now, you might have a question in your mind as to why I am making you do this exercise when technically, the purpose of a back cover blurb is to entice a shopper to buy the book when it's on a bookshelf in a bookstore. You're not wrong! Your book is going to be "print on demand," which means someone has to actually demand it, probably without reading the back cover.

I have several reasons for still putting the back cover blurb on self-published books. For one, I believe that self-published books should maintain the level of professionalism of traditionally published books from big publishing houses, mostly because I don't want trad publishers thinking we can't do things just as well as they can! Traditionally published books have back cover blurbs, and yours should too. Don't sell your book short just because you're putting it out yourself! The back of your book will be visible on Amazon when the "Look Inside" feature is turned on, and some people do read that!

Ultimately, your back cover is not going to help you sell books in the traditional sense because, as we noted, your book is unlikely to be in physical bookstores (at least initially), but that doesn't mean it won't help you in the long run. Think about it: when people will buy your book on Amazon, that means it'll be out in the world sitting in people's houses, or in libraries and classrooms. You'll want everyone who picks up the book to want to read it, and, ideally, what's on your back cover will entice them to do just that. Think of it as a little advertisement, one that should be a great representation not only of your book, but of you as an author!

I am also going to take this opportunity to get up on my "books are business" soapbox here and start yelling about how you need an author website. Fun! The back cover is yet another place where there should be a link to your author website. What if the person who picks up your book doesn't want that specific book but thinks you sound interesting as an author and would like to learn more about you? How will they do that if you don't have an author website with a prominent link on the back cover of your book?

That is just a sad missed opportunity right there, and I don't want that for you. Food for thought!

Returning to our fill-in-the-blank exercise, we are now getting to the "Why and the How" of your book, so fill in some more of these blanks using some of the keywords you found when you were researching:

"My book is about _____, and here is a little more detail about that." (Ideally, this paragraph will convince people they cannot live without this book):

_____

_____

_____

Next, add a little more about you as an author, perhaps including why you're qualified to write this book. Don't forget to include a link to your fantastic author website that I will never stop mentioning:

_____

_____

_____

_____

. . .

If you're now having a writer's block attack for what to put on the back cover and this exercise has not helped you break through it, go around your house, pull out a couple of books on your bookshelf, read through their back-cover blurbs, then come back and bang out one for your book. Try not to overthink this!

Description

We're now going to further expand your summary/blurb and turn it into a book description for Amazon. Unlike the first two, your description is something that customers can definitely read, so we'll want to tailor it to be a little more sales-y.

Oh, and just to get this out of the way, you might have heard from one or more YouTube publishing gurus that Amazon doesn't actually index your book's description, so it doesn't matter if you fill this space or not. I think this is really bad advice, and I will tell you why.

By "index," I mean read, remember, and return your book for searched words that appear in your description. Amazon is essentially a search engine for books, so there has been a lot of debate recently over whether to really blow out the description with keywords, to use it as a sales page (because it's customer facing), or to leave it mostly blank because it doesn't really help you get found in Amazon's algorithm.

Here's where I land on this: Amazon doesn't release official information about their algorithm, so no one knows for 100% sure that the description text isn't being indexed (or if they're going to start indexing it in the future), but the bottom line is, I just don't think you should waste any real estate that Amazon gives you.

Also, even though Amazon's internal search engine might not index your description text, you know who does? Google. Your book may turn up in Google searches for whatever keywords you put in that box, so for that reason alone, I would try to make the most out of the description.

But the other (perhaps most important!) reason to write a great description is the customer experience. Why would you not use that space to try to convince someone to buy your book? Yes, most of the description is technically "below the fold," but on the off chance that one person scrolls all the way down there, I say just go ahead and tell them a little more about your book and why they can't live without it. What if that person becomes your superfan and gets you a million-dollar publishing deal?

Okay. Now that I've told you **why** I try to use up that description space, let me tell you what you can put in there so you aren't staring at a blank 4,000 character box. I will go through this for fiction and non-fiction, because they're a little different.

First, pull out the competitive analysis research that you did back in Chapter 3. Click the link for each book in your competitive analysis list, scroll all the way down, and read all of their descriptions. That's going to take a minute and is hopefully going to give you a lot of ideas about your own work, so open up a new word processing document (or pull out your notebook).

. . .

For fiction, you'll want to include a great description of the plot and the characters, starting with whatever hook draws people into the book. If you've already written the back matter for the book jacket, you'll definitely want to include that and expand upon it to create this description. I would also recommend including some of the keywords that you unearthed during the keyword research section and that you think best describe your book's genre or category (like "cozy mysteries," "chick lit," "paranormal fiction," and so on). Definitely refer back to your competitors' books that you studied in the competitive analysis chapter, the keywords you compiled from the keyword research chapter, and even the categories you discovered while you were doing that research.

For non-fiction, it's a little easier to write a book description because you can do a lot more keyword research. You wrote that book to solve a problem, so you probably have a good idea of what you should be saying to try to sell it.

If it'll fit, I would include the whole table of contents (you can feel free to put it in bullet point form so it looks a little nicer on the page). Doing this will almost certainly guarantee that you hit a lot of your good keywords. If you read my book on making websites, you'll recognize this as my "latent semantic indexing" strategy.

Another thing I would do for a non-fiction description is open with one or more questions that identify the problem someone may be having and to tell the reader how you're going to solve that problem.

. . .

Here is a snazzy example of a description I would write for a book about women's weight loss after 40:

Did you reach age 40, only to find that you can no longer lose weight? Are you eating fewer calories than ever but noticing that the scale is not budging? Do you wish someone could tell you what to eat already?

If you are struggling with middle-age weight gain, this book is for you. After five years tracking and experimenting with her own weight, [author name] cracked the code, finding that she could eat what she wanted again and still maintain her high-school weight.

I would then go on to describe some of the weight-loss techniques in the book, stick the table of contents in there, and then go on a little about the author as a weight loss expert and person who has personally solved this problem.

(By the way, if you actually have written a book cracking the code for women's weight loss after 40, please feel free to take this concept and description and use it, with my compliments!)

One important note: whereas I will harass you to put your author website everywhere on God's green earth, one place you should not put it is in your Amazon book description. Amazon does not like it when people self-promote, so they are not going to be amused if they find you telling people to visit a totally different website in the listing for your book. There actually is a place to include your website (and blog) on your Amazon Author page, so go ahead and put it there, but leave it out of the actual description. (Definitely include that biographical info about yourself, though!)

· · ·

In closing, yes, you do need a summary, blurb, and description for your book, and now is the time to write those. In fact, you're going to need the back cover blurb three chapters from now when you hire your designer, so make sure it's done before you move on!

7
THE MARKETING BARE MINIMUM

Hey, remember in Chapter 1 when I mentioned how you'd need to decide whether you're putting this book out for fun or you're wanting to start your career as a working author, and how this moment would be a crossroads for you?

This is that moment.

Now that you're organized and have all of your prep and research done, we need to have a little marketing talk. Believe me, I don't want to do this either, but any later is going to be too late because we're about to jump into formatting.

You can feel free to skip this chapter if the only thing you want is to see your book in print and you truly don't care if you ever sell a copy. Be honest with yourself, though. I find that 99% of authors would actually *love* to write full time and have people buy their books, but they either don't know what to do, or they get immediately overwhelmed and give up when they think about the whole concept of their "author platforms." I know that's too much to talk about right now since you're just about to publish your first book and you might want to work on all of this later, so I want to give you my best piece of marketing advice right here. Putting this one thing in place right now is going to put you miles ahead of every other author who is self-publishing.

That thing is your email list.

Side note: If you already have an email list, you are fantastic and I am totally proud of you! The TL;DR of this chapter is that you also need a landing page with a free offer to get people to sign up for that list (which you can make inside your email marketing service), and you'll need to put the link to that landing page inside the book you're working on right now since you're just about to format it. If you have those pieces in place and you're ready to go with that link, you're golden! Move right on to interior formatting.

If all of that sounded crazy to you because you don't even know what an email marketing service is yet, that is totally fine, but we need to stop what we're doing right now and get you up to speed with a concept I call the "marketing bare minimum" for independent publishers like us.

For me (and my clients), the marketing bare minimum for a self-published book consists of two email list-related things I want all authors to have from the very beginning, even if they have no author website and no social media. Those things are: *a place for your list to live (this is called an email marketing service) and a way to get people onto that list.*

Why do I think you need to stop what you're doing and set this email thing up right now instead of waiting until you have your book launched? I'll tell you.

Because the best time to recruit someone for your list *is when they're actually reading your book*! And the best way to do this is to place a link in your book offering them some awesome thing in exchange for joining your email list. You want to get them when they're hot!

If you don't set this up now, you're going to be starting from scratch with every single launch. If you don't set this up now, you run the risk of being one of those authors who is constantly hanging out in Facebook groups going, "I published my book, but no one is buying it! How can I promote my book?" If you don't set this up now, you are going to get caught up in the excitement of publishing your book, only to find that you missed this huge opportunity.

Oh, and in case you're about to make the argument that you don't have a list because lists are old-school and you have a bunch of followers on social media, allow me to disagree. You do not actually own anything on your social media. Instagram, TikTok, Facebook, Twitter are all for-profit companies, and they are not going to mind taking away every single one of your followers if something you're doing interferes with their bottom line. With an email list, your people belong to you, and you can reach them (in their actual email inboxes!) anytime you want. No one has control of that communication but you.

Now that I've (hopefully) convinced you that you do need an email list and that now is the time to start building it (and I *have* convinced you, haven't I?!), you're probably wondering how this all works.

Here's how: What you're going to do is offer people something awesome (like, say, some supplementary material for whatever they're already reading) in exchange for becoming your fan and signing up for your list. Again, you are making that offer *inside your actual book* by including a link to a landing page with that offer and email signup.

So there's no confusion, I am not talking about the box on your author website (if you have one, and you really should have one) where you try to get people to subscribe to your newsletter. I'm talking about offering your reader, who is reading your book, something really valuable, which is represented by a link that appears in the book itself.

Like this:

https://loriculwell.com/sellmorebooks

"Wow," you're thinking. "That sounds like a lot of extra work. I bought this book because I just want to self-publish my book. Leave me alone! I'll do this later."

I get it, but we have to do this right now. There is no "later." You need the landing page link to put inside your manuscript. You need this whole thing set up BEFORE you publish your first book, and trust me here—you will be sorry if you don't do it. If you get all the way through the self-publishing process and don't have that all-important link inside your book, every single sale you make is a wasted opportunity to gain a new fan.

Every single sale!

. . .

I don't know how you're currently planning to get people to actually buy your book when you launch it (paid advertising, referrals, Amazon suggestions, witchcraft, some other suggestions I put into chapter 20), but you absolutely must give those people the chance to get on your list right then, or you're going to be re-inventing the wheel with every single launch. You don't want that! If someone buys your book and likes it enough to actually click the link inside of it to get a free thing, you OWE it to yourself as an author to give that person an opportunity to become your fan.

Also, good news! I feel so passionately about this subject, I actually stopped writing this book and spent an entire week writing a supplementary guide on this subject, just for you. In it, I focus on getting your head around the very concept of email marketing, which is going to mean familiarizing yourself with a bunch of jargon, picking the right email marketing service, and getting everything set up properly so you have that all-important link to put in your manuscript. That guide is called "Funny You Should Ask: How to Sell More Books" and you can get your free copy at https://loriculwell.com/sellmorebooks

By the way, I feel the need to point out that I am doing the very thing I'm talking about, right now, right here, in front of your face. You know those pictures that are a picture of a guy in a picture that's the same guy inside the picture and so on and so on until your brain explodes? Yeah, this is that.

Anyway, I want you to stop and do this process so badly, I made the whole thing free—the ebook itself is free, and I only covered services that offer free accounts, even though one of them required me to use a lame workaround that made me want to scream. I did a super detailed walkthrough of not one, not two, but THREE different email marketing services (and how to make a landing page and a welcome email delivering the freebie at each one) because I wanted to give you ample choices and instructions. My goal with this book (and that ebook) is to send you out into the world with your first self-published book, and to my thinking, your book isn't complete unless it has that landing page link inside of it to start growing your list.

You have to have that link because the link is the beginning of your list, and your list is the beginning of your life as a working author.

I know this whole chapter has been jarring, and I'm really sorry to take us off track like this, but you would simply not believe how many authors I talk to who have 10, 20, or even 50 books and have never even heard of or considered an email list. That is a rough conversation, and I don't want that to be you in the future! Almost all of those authors (once they stop being upset and defensive) say something to the effect of, "I wish someone had told me this before I published my first book." It's for this reason that I decided to have this talk with every author at the *beginning* of their self-publishing journey.

In conclusion—please, PLEASE go get your free copy of the "How to Sell More Books" guide at https://loriculwell.com/sellmore books , pick an email service, set up the giveaway, and come back here with that link for the inside of your book. I cannot make it any clearer: YOU WILL BE SORRY if you don't start thinking about your list right now. Don't say I didn't warn you!

Okay, good talk. Go and read that ebook, and when you have the link to your landing page ready, move on to formatting!

On the other hand, if you have had that "crossroads" moment and have decided you're only publishing your book for yourself and friends, that is also fine. You can move on to formatting!

8

TRIM SIZE/INTERIOR FORMATTING FOR PRINT

Here we are, finally! Formatting your book for upload into the KDP system! Now we're getting somewhere!

This is the process for formatting the interior of your book's manuscript for print (meaning, paperback and hardcover). If you want to do the ebook first, that is covered in the next chapter and it's totally fine to do that, but be sure to come back here and do this process, because you definitely want printed versions of your books for sale! I do print formatting first because I always upload the print version first, but that's just me.

One of the biggest decisions you'll need to make at the beginning of the publishing process is what *trim size* you're going to want your book to be. Amazon can publish your book in a bunch of different sizes, and it is your job to decide which size you want and then to bring an appropriately formatted manuscript in those dimensions to the upload process.

Just to reiterate: *Amazon does not resize your manuscript* during the upload process. If you tell it you want your book to be 6 X 9, but if you give it a manuscript that is still 8.5 X 11, that's going to be a mess.

The scenario above, simple as it might seem, is probably the one I hear the most from authors who are self-publishing for the first time. I feel like it is not spelled out quite clearly enough in the actual KDP upload interface, so you only learn that you needed to format the book for a certain size when they tell you the size you've uploaded is wrong. That is what we call the rudest of rude awakenings right there.

Also, you'll need to get your trim size nailed down before you start working on the cover design, because guess what? The size of a full-width cover is based on page count. If you've been writing your book in a standard size (8.5 X 11) Word doc and want to publish it as a 6 X 9 trim size, your book is going to end up something like 30% more pages than you think it is right now. Finding this out too late is going to increase the amount of hours your designer has to put into your cover, which will increase your cost basis for the book.

Just to circumvent that frustrating scenario, let's just make sure your manuscript is sized and formatted properly so it sails through the upload process, shall we?

. . .

First, pull out your competitive analysis from the beginning of the book (here I go again with that!) and take a look at the average size of the books in your genre and category. You'll want to choose a size that is roughly analogous to the others because that is what readers expect when they buy a book in that niche. What I'm saying is: if every poetry book in your genre is 6 X 9 and you decide to make yours 8.5 x 11 just to stand out, you are probably going to get some angry reviews about that.

So, what size should you choose? I would recommend not only looking at all of the titles in your competitive analysis to see what the standard size is for your genre/category, but also walking around your house to see what book sizes appeal to you.

As I mentioned, 6 x 9 is usually the standard default so you're probably fine going with that (especially for your very first book), but if your book is a little pocket-size book of some kind of wisdom and you'd like it to be 5 X 8, go for it!

This is when I will stop and HIGHLY RECOMMEND that you pick from the following sizes, because these are the sizes that Amazon can also do in hardcover form. This will keep you from having to resize the manuscript when you get to the hardcover upload (you're still going to need a totally different cover, though). For instance, if you haven't formatted your book yet and you want your book to be 8 X 10, but you're actually fine having it be 7 X 10, definitely go with the latter, because 7 X 10 can be done in hardcover form.

For reference, here's the hardcover chart:

Hardcover
Trim Size
5.5" x 8.5" (13.97 x 21.59 cm)
6" x 9" (15.24 x 22.86 cm)
6.14" x 9.21" (15.6 x 23.39 cm)
7" x 10" (17.78 x 25.4 cm)
8.25" x 11" (20.96 x 27.94 cm)

Sizes Not Eligible for Expanded Distribution (another totally random side note):

This is another one of those things Amazon should tell you upfront but does not. Because of printer limitations in other countries, if you choose certain sizes and paper types for your book, that book will not be available for expanded distribution. That means you'll need to prepare yourself for the fact that the high-concept square book you're about to spend so long designing is only going to have limited (meaning, only in the U.S.) distribution in paperback form, and none at all in hardcover. Chances are you're not going to care about this if you're trying to self-publish a high-concept book like that. Still, I'm trying to cover every question or scenario that might come up when you're publishing, so I thought I would put it out there now, before your book is formatted.

Formatting Your Interior

Once you've decided on what your trim size will be, you'll need to make sure it is properly formatted so it will be approved by Amazon and be ready to be printed as a physical book.

If your book is mostly words and very few images, you can most likely get away with a word processing document by just turning page numbers on, changing the size in the Page Setup, reformatting the headings, and making sure everything looks the way you want it. This is will probably be the scenario for most people who are reading this book, and it is definitely the simplest, so I will cover it first.

Here's where you change the page size in Word. If you use Pages, Google Docs, or another word processing program, this will probably look a little bit different, but you get the idea.

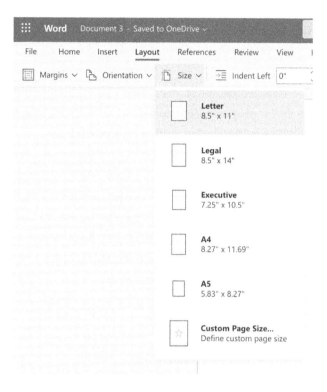

Select "custom page size," then change the dimensions to match whatever trim size you've decided on, like this:

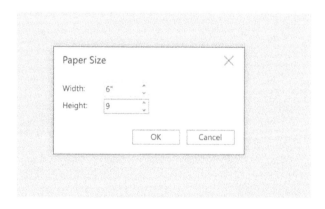

Once you've changed the page size to your preferred trim size, your document will go and re-configure itself, emerging anew with more (a lot more!) pages.

Take that moment to be proud of yourself for writing a much longer book than you thought! You are awesome!

You'll then need to go back through the document and do the following:

— Add the copyright page to the front matter. You can find guidelines and samples over at: https://kindlepreneur.com/book-copyright-page-examples-ebook/

— Add the landing page link for the freebie/ email signup to the front, back, and anywhere else in the manuscript it fits.

— make sure the spacing is right (I go with 1.2)

— make sure the font size looks the way you want it to (12 point Times usually looks good, but that is totally up to you), the chapter headings are in the right place, and the table of contents corresponds with the correct page numbers.

—add page numbers to the whole document.

. . .

You'll also need to do an "Insert Page" where necessary so that all chapters start on an ODD page number (the odd page is the one that appears on the right-hand side in KDP). You might also want to export the whole thing to pdf. KDP will take documents from some word processing programs but not others, but pdfs are universal, so you're better off with that as your final product.

That should be it! If your book is all or mostly words, you'll probably be fine. Just make sure you complete all of these steps before ordering your cover, because you'll need that exact page count for the full-width cover dimensions.

If you do all of this and you find that you're still not happy with how the interior layout looks (some authors are never happy with how a book in a word processing document looks), come on back here and we'll talk about some of the more advanced methods of formatting an interior. There is always a way!

More Complex Formatting

If your book has images or complex formatting of any kind (like this one does, for instance), it will need to be laid out using a software program (several examples coming) so that you can ensure that each image stays where you put it. If you've ever tried to deal with images in a word processing document, you have probably felt the pain of making one change (like adding a page break), only to have all of your formatting completely fall apart because the text that goes with the images keeps sliding around everywhere. My experience with this is that if you have images in the book, you're probably not going to get it to be print-quality just with a word processing doc, but your mileage may vary!

Professional book industry people will say that the only solution is to bite the bullet and learn an actual publishing layout software like Adobe InDesign (or its lower-priced equivalent, Affinity Publisher), and they are not wrong! I suppose if you have created a super complex and fancy book interior, you might already know one of those, so definitely go with that!

This will to make designers cringe, but another (super DIY) way I have found to lay out a book interior is by using a presentation software like PowerPoint or Keynote, both of which can be exported as a pdf. Just make sure you have the right dimensions for the trim size you've selected (Keynote makes you convert this into *points*, which is a little weird).

I'm working on my InDesign skills in my copious free time, but as I am still unable to successfully format a book without crying, I finally invested in the "print formatting" upgrade of Vellum, (the software I use to format ebooks) and am currently using that for print book formatting. It actually works surprisingly well with screenshots and images! You can find that over at www. vellum.com.

That's everything I want you to know about print interior formatting. Since we've now opened up the topic of ebooks, let's go ahead and talk about it!

9
FORMATTING YOUR EBOOK

This is one of those moments when I am going to tell you something you probably didn't know and most likely won't want to hear.

What a delightful way to start off a chapter! Believe me, there was no other way, so I decided to just rip the Band-Aid off and start talking about this. Honestly, I'm introducing this topic now (rather than further into the upload process) because I want you to have ample time to get your head around this concept and do something about it before you get to the actual upload.

Here's the deal: your book is going to need to be properly formatted as an ebook before you upload it into KDP (or anywhere else, for that matter). Your word processing doc is most likely not going to cut it.

. . .

Maybe you already knew this, and now you think I'm being overdramatic. That's fine. This is something you've come to expect from me by now.

Here's the thing—I've talked to many, many authors who think you can just take your word processing document and throw it into the KDP system as is. They think that Amazon/KDP is going to do the necessary conversion to make their book look like the Kindle ebooks they are familiar with, complete with functional navigation (linked table of contents, proper formatting for electronic reading, and clickable links that go to websites).

Sadly, that is not true, and because Amazon doesn't make that clear, I am now the messenger who has to tell you (please don't shoot me!). Exactly like how you have to pre-format the paperback before you upload it for printing, ebook formatting is something you either have to do yourself or pay someone to do well before you hit the upload process for the book to exist as a professional-looking Kindle book.

You'd think that because Amazon wants you to put your books on their marketplace, they would let you just take your word processing document and convert it for you, and you're totally right! It would make perfect sense for them to do that!

And yet, here we are. Formatting the ebook can honestly be one of the most mysteriously frustrating parts of this entire process, which is why I am going to give you a general overview of what your finished product will need to contain, as well as several ways for you to get there.

. . .

As I mentioned, the most important thing you're trying to do with your Kindle book formatting is to make sure all of the interior elements are where you want them, that the table of contents is linked to the chapters, and that all external links (like that all-important link back to your author website) are clickable.

Here, for want of a better term, is the "manual" way to do this yourself in order to get your manuscript to meet the bare minimum requirements for Kindle, using whatever word processing document you've used to write your book. I'm giving you this workaround because I totally understand that ebook formatting is something you only just learned about and that you are going to need time to get your head around it—plus you might just want to move on from all of this prep so you can get to the upload phase. The beauty of self-publishing is that it is iterative, so you can make improvements at any time!

The Most Basic DIY ebook Formatting Instructions: Try This First

I will say up front that if you do this and your book still doesn't look good in Kindle form once you get to the upload section, you'll need to use one of the more advanced methods I have listed below (or contact me for the name of the formatting guy I have used).

What you'll need to do is go through your entire document page by page and do the following:

. . .

—put the Kindle book cover you got from your designer in the beginning of the manuscript (you might need to come back to this later, especially if you have just finished the chapter on hiring a designer and are waiting for the cover to be done).

—manually designate all chapter titles as headers.

—justify all of the text on each page so that it is equally aligned to the right and left.

—insert a page break at the end of every chapter.

—make sure all links are live, meaning they are clickable and go to an actual website. This is actually a combination of formatting and quality control, but it has to be done at some point, so you might as well just get it over with now.

—go back up to the beginning of the document and generate a custom table of contents (which will be pulled from the headers you designated). You'll want "show hyperlinks" instead of page numbers.

—save or export the entire file as docx.

Ideally, this will be the most you'll have to do to your file, and it will look great when you upload it and preview it in Chapter 12.

.   .   .

If it doesn't (or if you're taking my advice and distributing your book to platforms other than Amazon and therefore need an ePub version of your book), come on back to this chapter and read further.

Pro Converting/Formatting: More Resources

Okay, you're either reading this because you formatted your manuscript in word-processing-document form, uploaded it, and then didn't like the way it looked; or you've discovered that you need it in different formats for wider distribution purposes. Either way, now is the time to learn about the different services and pieces of software that can help you format it properly.

One important thing to understand is that you're not just trying to convert the file (i.e., running the file through a piece of software that turns your .docx file into an .ePub so you can get this over with already). Doing that would just take the same problems you had in the word-processing version of the document and convert them over (while probably messing the manuscript up even more), and that's not what you want.

Now, you may be tempted to Google "convert my ebook for Kindle" because that makes sense, and you're a rational person. The problem is, you're likely to find advice on doing the conversion precisely how I just advised you not to do it. What you actually need is software for conversion and formatting. That is to say, you need to convert your word processing document into a form where you can properly format it, then export it into a proper ebook file. The difference is subtle but important.

· · ·

The first place to go is Amazon itself. Their free Kindle Create software is what they are currently recommending you use to convert, format, and export your ebook so that it has the proper functional navigation for their system.

You can find Kindle Create here: https://www.amazon.com/Kindle-Create/b?ie=UTF8&node=18292298011

And here's a handy tutorial to get you started: https://kdp.amazon.com/en_US/help/topic/GYVL2CASGU9ACFVU

Note: this software is Kindle-only, meaning it only produces a KPF file suitable for upload into its own ecosystem. If you want to branch out and publish on other platforms, you will need to use different software (which I cover below) to format and export into the required ePub files. Because, really, did we expect Amazon to help us publish our books elsewhere? We did not.

. . .

As promised, here are some other options for formatting your book properly and exporting it as an ePub.

Vellum (https://vellum.pub)

Vellum is the go-to software of many self-publishing types because it's stand-alone and easy to use. Just for the purposes of this book (because I try to practice what I preach, people!), I bought Vellum and taught myself how to use it, and now I completely love it and it is my number-one recommendation. I am pleased to announce that I have successfully formatted an ebook for the first time in my writing career! Shockingly, once I got the hang of it, I found the process to be actually enjoyable, which is something I never thought I would say. I'm growing as a person! I no longer rant about ebook formatting, and I love Vellum so much I now also use it for print interiors.

Just so you know, Vellum is a paid software ($199.99 for ebooks only, $249.99 for ebooks and print), which does seem pricey until you consider the fact that it costs about $100 to pay someone to convert your book into perfect ebook form for you. Do this a couple of times and you'll have already justified the cost of this investment.

You can download Vellum for free to try it out, then pay the one-time fee for lifetime access if you love it and decide you're going to use it to format all of your books from now on. FYI, it is Mac-only (sorry, PC people!)

Atticus
   http://atticus.io

If you don't like Kindle Create (I'm right there with you!) and don't use Mac or don't want to invest in Vellum, your next move is to check out atticus.io, which is Dave Chesson's new writing and formatting software. Dave, you'll recall, is the genius behind Publisher Rocket, and he has now branched out into writing and formatting tools.

I bought Atticus and tested it extensively so I could rate it and give you my recommendation. Here it is: so far, I really like it as a writing and formatting tool, and I think it's well-priced and would totally work for you if you're developing an original project (like, say, the book you're trying to format right now).

It costs less than Vellum (currently $147), has more formatting options, and works on Mac and PC. Yes, Atticus is still pretty new, and they are still working out the bugs of some of the features, but I was able to successfully format and export an entire ebook without too much hassle, which is the ultimate goal.

One caveat: I did not find the import function to work well at all, and this was confirmed by the Atticus team as something that is still "in development" even though it is mentioned on their sales page as a feature that is currently working. This function would apply to you only if you wanted to import existing ebooks and edit them yourself going forward. I don't imagine many of you would, but it's something I wanted to warn you about.

To recap: I tested both Vellum and Atticus, and I'm enjoying both of them, but Vellum is my number-one recommendation. Either (or both) would be great options for you in terms of formatting your ebook—and this is definitely a skill you'll need to develop at some point if you're going to continue self-publishing books.

Another option is Reedsy, which you can find at www.reedsy.com:

Here's the book editor:

https://reedsy.com/write-a-book

Here's the tutorial:

https://blog.reedsy.com/how-to-format-a-book/

Honestly, the only reason this Reedsy tool isn't my number-one recommendation is because I find their website to be a little diffi-cult to navigate since it's also a talent marketplace. It seems too easy to end up back in the talent directory when you're just trying to format your ebook properly and move on with your life.

I don't want to say Reedsy offers you this nifty free editor while expecting you to give up and hire one of their experts, but that is what the information architecture of the website itself would suggest (to me, at least). And let's be clear—I'm not saying you shouldn't hire experts from Reedsy. They're great. I am saying, however, that if you're going to spend Reedsy-type money, I think it should be on services like editors, proofreaders, and designers.

If you've had a look at these options and have decided that you're too exhausted for this crap right now and that you would rather spend the money hiring someone to do your ebook conversion, I feel you and am happy to give you my guy's name and contact info. Just reach out to me at www.loriculwell.com . (I'm not trying to pull a bait-and-switch on you here; I just don't want to overwhelm this guy by printing his name in a book. That's fair, right?)

Well! That's it for "everything you never wanted to know about ebook conversion and formatting but were afraid to ask." This is a lot to learn, and you're doing great!

10

COVER DESIGN

Now that you have your interior finalized and formatted and know your final page count (and maybe even have your manuscript out to some early reviewers from your email list), you can turn your attention to your cover design.

Your cover is one of the most important parts (if not *the* most important part) of your entire book. If the cover is bad, it's going to be really hard to get that book to be successful, even if it is filled with amazing prose and insights. A bad cover is the thing that will cause a book to fail, followed by poor (or no) marketing and lack of proper metadata.

When you think about it, this makes total sense because the cover (and often, the thumbnail of the cover) is your one and only chance to catch the reader's eye, which will hopefully lead them to read the description, which will hopefully lead them to buy the book. Your book's cover must be great! If you're going to spend money, spend it on this!

Now that I've raised the stakes on how important that cover is to the overall success of your book (SO IMPORTANT!), let's get started on your cover design process.

It's time to pull out that competitive analysis you did of the top 5-10 books that are similar to yours and take a look at them to give you some design guidance for your cover.

The first question everyone always asks me at this point is: "Should I design the cover myself?"

That is a great question, and I will answer it with another question. Are you a designer? If so, definitely design your own cover! That's going to save you a ton of money! You can totally skim this chapter. There is a link to the cover dimensions calculator at the end, and you'll need that to generate your templates.

If not—and I cannot emphasize this enough—*spend the money (or barter with designer friends) to have an actual designer make your cover.* You will never get a second chance to make that perfect first impression (especially when your book first comes out and Amazon is showing it to the maximum amount of potential buyers), plus you are not going to enjoy how long it takes you to get all the dimensions just right to comply with Amazon's upload requirements. This is the kind of thing that doesn't phase designers one bit.

. . .

Look, I'm not telling you to work with a designer because it gets me anything. I'm not a designer! I actually don't care what you put on your cover. But since you put all of that energy into writing that book, getting it copyedited and proofread, doing keyword and category research, getting your email list set up, and formatting the interior, it would be a cryin' shame to not sell any copies because your cover looks like you threw it together in Microsoft Paint.

That's a real thing that happens to authors that I talk to. Great book + bad cover = being super sad and discouraged.

Hiring and Working with a Designer

Before you start looking for a designer, make sure you have a) decided on the trim size you're going to want the book to be, b) finalized formatting of the book's interior (and the page count) so you can give the designer specific dimensions, c) written the blurb for the back cover, and d) performed the competitive analysis, so you have a vague idea of what you're going to want the designer to do with your cover. Some designers will not take the project without all of these things, so make sure you've done your homework!

You don't have to put a whole design brief together, but you do need some idea of what you want. if you approach a design process going, "I don't know—do whatever *you* think is best," two things will happen. First, you will end up overpaying because of all the iterations and revisions you're going to request, and second, you and the designer will both end up aggravated, and no one wants that!

Therefore, right now, before we go any further, take out some paper (or open up a file on your computer), pull out all of your notes, and start writing some stuff down. In fact, answer these questions I've laid out below. You're going to end up answering them anyway once you find a designer. I promise you it is cheaper for you to sit and answer them now as opposed to waiting until you sign a contract and then paying the designer to pull these answers out of you (or worse, paying for a design that you end up hating because you didn't refine your vision before you started the process).

Questions to Answer/Things to Do Before You Hire a Designer

Purpose/Functionality
You can probably pull most of this from the work you did on your keywords and your book description/ blurb. Repurposing for the win!

1. What is your book about?

2. Who is the target audience/demographic for your book?

3. No, really. Who did you write this book for? Please don't say everyone. That is almost never true.

Look/Feel

4. Take the screenshots of each book cover on your list of 5-10 books from your competitive analysis and open them up all at once.

5. Of those, which ones do you like the most? Spend some time really looking at them and writing down what you like about them. Do you like the color combinations? Your cover doesn't have to look exactly like theirs (and in fact, it shouldn't!), but you're going to want to fit in with the general vibe/theme that is already selling in that category. Do not try to re-invent the wheel with your first self-published book, especially if you don't have a ton of people on your email list (yet) to externally stimulate your sales.

6. Do you have a color palette (or design look and feel) in mind based on the niche or genre of your book? For example, have you noticed that all other meditation books have images of lotus flowers on them? Make a note of that.

Budget

What is your total budget for the cover design? Please write this down so that you know it, but *do not* say this number to the designer initially. This is just for your reference, so you can compare it to the quotes you get from other designers you interview.

Timing

What is your desired launch date for your book? Does this date work with the designer's schedule? How long will revisions take, and how many are included in the fee for the project? Is it going to cost more if you add quotes (or other extras) or change your page count after the fact? Talk about all of this up front.

Are you absolutely certain that your book (and especially the trim size, interior formatting, and page count) are finalized? Once you hire the designer and give them the specifications, you are officially done fiddling around with the words inside the book. Every time you make a change after that, that's on you, and it's going to cost extra.

Great! Now that you have all of that written down (or you've at least thought about it), you'll be in good shape to start looking around for a designer.

Print Cover Calculator and Templates

To find out the exact dimensions of your cover, use the calculator. You can also download a template (PDF and PNG) to be used as a guide layer in your image editing software. Learn more about Hardcover and Paperback cover requirements.

Enter Your Book Information

Binding type

Select one ⌄

Interior type

Select one

Paper type

Select one

Page-turn direction

Select one

Measurement units

Select one

Interior trim size

Select one

Page count
Number of pages at your formatted trim size.
Learn more about trim size and page count

Calculate dimensions

Download Template

Reset book information

Dimensions and Specifications

Here's some information about the cover dimensions for your Kindle **eBook cover:**

—The image for your Kindle eBook cover will need to be a .tiff or a .jpeg

—Ideal dimensions for your cover file are 2560 X 1600 (2560 pixels high x 1600 pixels wide).

•   •   •

—Cover file must be at least 1000 X 625 (1000 pixels high x 625 pixels wide)

Here is the place to get the exact dimensions (and even templates!) for the paperback and hardcover versions of your book (which are going to be two different sizes even though the trim size is the same). Go over there and generate the templates, so you can provide them to your designer when you hire them.

https://kdp.amazon.com/cover-calculator

This is the (brand new!) cover calculator. It works for both paperback and hardcover. Just fill in your book's info, click "calculate dimensions," and you'll be good to go!

Yes, this is a lot of information you have to know right off the bat, but don't panic! You've got this.

For the average book, 9 times out of 10, you're going to want the following specifications:
    —paper type: "white"
    —interior type: "black and white"
    —page-turn direction: "left to right"
    —measurement units: "inches"
    —trim size: whatever you chose (probably 6 x 9)

I will advise you not to choose the cream paper. It looks really nice, but it will limit your expanded distribution options in some areas (something you won't find out until it's too late). Save the cream paper for a specialty project where you are more concerned about aesthetics. Yes, the "Cover Design" section seems like a weird place to decide what kind of paper your book is going to have, but cream paper is actually thicker than white, so this choice will impact the overall size of your cover and is going to jam you up later (in the upload section) if you change it.

When you hit the "calculate dimensions" button, you'll get a zip file containing a .png and a pdf, either of which your designer (or you!) can use to create your perfectly sized cover. You'll need to have the pdf of your cover ready to go before you start the upload section. You will need to repeat this process twice: once for the paperback, and once for the hardcover.

The only thing left for you to do is provide the designer with a photo of yourself (if you want one of those on there), plus the blurb for the back cover, which, of course, is a roughly 250-word description of what your book is about.

If you don't have that blurb written yet, I would encourage you to stop and get that done right now. You probably wrote something like this in your answer to my "Questions to Ask Yourself/Things to Do Before You Hire a Designer" list, so now you can expand upon and repurpose it. You'll need it in several other places, including the big "book description" that Amazon requires during the upload process and in your marketing materials.

Once you hire the designer, the heavy lifting (for you) is over. You'll just need to wait for them to finish it and deliver it to you before starting the upload process. Your designer will probably already know this, but just to be safe, please let them know you will need the following files:

—ebook: jpeg or tiff

—paperback: print-ready PDF

—hardcover: print-ready PDF

So you know, "print-ready" is a much higher resolution than a regular pdf, and you'll need that for your cover to look good in printed form. Your designer will probably know this, but it never hurts to reconfirm!

Finding and Hiring a Designer

Let's find you a designer! You might already know someone, or you may be able to find somebody just by asking around a little bit, but if you're having trouble, here are some suggestions for places you can look:

1. Ask your friends and colleagues. This is my first go-to method, and it usually works. If someone you know has a great-looking book, ask them whom they used and whether they had a good experience.

2. Ask around locally. If you belong to a neighborhood or city group on Facebook or NextDoor, ask for names of local designers. Not only is it nice to support your community, but it can be easier to get through a whole process of cover design and revisions if you can have coffee with the designer in person.

. . .

3. Try Fiverr. If my first two methods didn't yield any designers (and I would be shocked if they didn't), go over to fiverr.com and search for "KDP Cover." There are some great designers over there who will make the ebook, paperback, and hardcover versions of your cover, and deliver them all at the same time.

4. Hire someone on 99Designs, Upwork, or 100Covers. There are some great designers over there who will make the ebook, paperback, and hardcover versions of your cover, and deliver them all at the same time.

5. If all else fails, do not despair. I can help! Go to loriculwell.com and get in touch with me via the "Contact Us" form. I will send you some references for designers (I have two that I use on Fiverr all the time). I don't necessarily want to link to them in this book for fear of inundating them, but I will totally send you over to them.

Okay, now that you've got your designer, what's next? First, you'll need to provide them with the exact dimensional requirements of the paperback and hardcover versions of your cover (which we calculated earlier).

Something to keep in mind: paperback and hardcover books are two totally different sizes, so you'll need two different PDFs. A word to the wise here: Do not try to save money by attempting to resize it yourself. Have your designer do it. I tried to do this once, and the results were laughably terrible.

. . .

Also, if it's at all possible, try not to finalize and close out the job until you have successfully uploaded both the paperback and hardcover versions of your book into the KDP system. I always prefer to structure design-type jobs in terms of "deposit, then payment upon final delivery," and you can't call it final delivery until you see that Amazon has accepted it with no errors.

Once your designer sends you the finalized files (again, jpeg/tiff for ebook, PDFs for paperback and hardcover), save those in a folder on your desktop. You will need to access them during the upload process, so you'll want them to be easily findable.

And there you have it—my general guidelines on how to find the exact dimensions of the cover, what exactly needs to be on the cover, and where to find a designer for the cover. I recognize I've already given you a lot to think about, but here are a few final dos and don'ts just to wrap this up and send you out into the world.

DO make sure your cover looks like it will fit in with the 5-10 most successful books on your competitive analysis list. Those successful books are appealing to your same target audience, so learn from what they're doing right!

DO make your cover look professional. Ideally, you have listened to my argument that this is a moment in your career where it's worth paying for a designer, but if you're designing your cover yourself (which is fine if you are a designer!), just make sure the title is centered and the cover doesn't look homemade.

·   ·   ·

DO have your book cover all ready to go in the right sizes for Kindle, paperback, and hardcover. You don't want the wrong size to cost you more money or hold up your launch!

DO look at your book cover in thumbnail form to make sure it looks okay. A lot of people look at Amazon only from their phones, so that cover is going to be tiny. Make sure it pops!

DO NOT scrimp on the cover. I know I'm overemphasizing this, but you spent a ton of time working on your book, so don't let a cheap cover sabotage it.

DO NOT finalize your job (meaning, do not release the designer) until you have successfully uploaded the pdfs of your paperback and hardcover into the system.

If you have no budget and don't know any designers at all, my last-ditch recommendation is to open a free Canva account and make your cover in there. Just make sure it looks comparable with the other books you found in your competitive analysis.

Now go forth and conquer!

PART 2: THE UPLOAD

Okay, here we are—the part where we actually start uploading your book into Amazon!

Believe me, I hear you cursing me, like, "Really, Culwell? HALFWAY through the book is when we start this?"

This is all about to make sense, I swear!

As I mentioned, I like to do the paperback version of my books first, so that's where we're starting. For this example, I'm going to walk you through uploading a book that is all text, in a word processing document (no photos or fancy formatting) with all of the default settings. (You'll see what I mean when we get there.)

Just so you know, Amazon is going to make you go through the upload process for all three versions of your book—the eBook, the paperback, and the hardcover, separately, but once you get through the first one, the other two are infinitely easier because they'll repurpose all of your work. I will be walking you through the Kindle and the paperback step by step since they have slightly different nuances. Hardcover is the exact same as paperback.

It's totally fine to skip over some (or all!) of these explanations if you don't want a detailed breakdown of that particular thing. My main goal with this guide is to answer every question I have ever heard from an author, thereby providing you with a one-stop-shop for answers so that you can just get yourself through the upload process. Remember, the first time's the hardest!

11
PAPERBACK DETAILS

Here we are, starting at the beginning of the beginning. This probably goes without saying, but the very first thing you'll need to do is open up a Kindle Direct Publishing (KDP) account, which you can do at kdp.amazon.com.

That looks like this:

If you have an Amazon account (like for ordering deodorant and socks), starting your KDP account is super easy. You're just going to click the yellow **"Sign In"** button at the top of the screen and proceed from there. Your KDP account is accessible by using your main Amazon login and password, so that's easy.

If you're the one person who still does not have an Amazon account after 25 years, I'm sorry, but you'll have to open one up just for publishing purposes. If being an Amazon holdout has been a point of pride for you, this is now your secret shame. You knew they would get you eventually!

Another note about Amazon and KDP: *You are allowed one KDP account, and one only!* It will be connected to your main Amazon ID, *so do not open multiple accounts* (even if you have multiple Amazon accounts for ordering things) and *do not log in to other people's accounts from your computer* (even if you end up loving publishing and want to do it for clients).

Yes, there were a lot of italics in that last paragraph, but this is *super important.* Having multiple KDP accounts violates Amazon's Terms of Service, and they will absolutely terminate you for this. I have heard horror stories about people losing their entire libraries because of problems with multiple accounts, so just *do not do this under any circumstances.* Amazon knows the IP address your account is logging in from (yes, that's somewhat creepy, let's just choose to ignore it), and they have no problem cutting you off if you cross them. Just a word of warning!

Now that you have your account, we'll start putting your book into the system. Click the big "+Create" button at the top of the page:

We're putting the paperback version of your book in first, so click the "Create Paperback" button to get started.

What would you like to create?

Pick an option and we'll get you started. You can save your progress as you go.
✔ Learn about the publishing process.

Kindle eBook

Publish digitally to Kindle and other hand-held devices. Includes comics and manga.

Create eBook

Paperback

Make your title available in print and ship around the world.

Create paperback

BETA
Hardcover

Bind your book in hardcover and ship around the world.

Create hardcover

Series page

Collect your books together and build a single Amazon Series page.

Create series page

NEW
Kindle Vella

Publish serialized stories to share with readers – one episode at a time.

Start a story

Pro Tip: After submitting your book, it can take up to 72 hours to appear on Amazon.com and up to 5 days for the remaining Amazon country websites. View other timelines.

In this section, we'll be tackling everything in the **"Paperback Details"** tab.

The first thing to decide is what language you're publishing this book in. For most people reading this guide, that language will be English, but if you're publishing in another language, find that language in the drop-down and select it. Amazon has a whole section about languages that are supported for paperbacks and ebooks, and if you are interested, you can find that here: https://kdp.amazon.com/en_US/help/topic/G200673300

I'm sure this goes without saying, but you'll need a totally different book listing for each language your book is in, so keep that in mind.

. . .

Next, we will start entering your book's metadata, which consists of your title, subtitle, description, and keywords. Make sure you have written your description and have done the keyword research and category research exercises in the prep portion of this guide before you hit this section! I'm warning you! I find that once authors get in here, the nerves take over and they just want to get it over with, so the prep work is key. If you don't do the prep, you're going to do your book a disservice. You are not going to want to stop and do a good job on your description, keywords, and category research once you are in there uploading your book. Don't proceed unless you've done the prep! We are about to start filling stuff in, for real!

For the **"Book Title"** field, you're going to put the title of the book the way it appears on either the cover and/or the spine. For traditional books, this is going to probably be the same thing, but I did want to let you know that if you have extra words on your cover (like a subtitle), you don't necessarily have to put those words in the "Book Title" field if the entire title appears on the spine. This can be super handy if you're publishing a book with a lot of words on the cover and you're wondering if you have to put them all in the title.

The answer is no. To Amazon, "Title" is whatever appears on the *spine*, so the cover can actually say something different.

Book Title   Enter your title as it appears on the book cover. This field cannot be changed after your book is published. Learn more about book
                  titles.

                  Book Title

                  Subtitle (Optional)

All that said, simplify your life by matching what you put in the "Book Title" field to the text on the spine. Trust me on this.

Okay, moving on to the subtitle. Believe it or not, your subtitle does not actually have to appear anywhere on your physical book. Some (spammy marketers) use this as an opportunity to repeat their keywords over and over in order to rank higher in the Amazon search (dumb example coming up!), but I don't think this helps, plus it seems to annoy Amazon.

This field is a point of contention and argument, with traditional publishing types on one side and hard-core marketing types on the other. Publishing die-hards will tell you that the subtitle must always appear on the book's cover and that you should really leave that field blank if you don't have a subtitle, and marketers will say, "WE NEVER LEAVE ANYTHING BLANK."

In the subtitle field, as in life, I fall somewhere between these two. I don't leave the subtitle field blank, but I try my best to make what I put in there relevant to the content of the book, and I will even include it on the cover if it goes with the design. I have tried it both ways, and I have found (anecdotally) that not including a subtitle at all does tend to negatively impact your book's ranking for keywords, which will ultimately impact its sales. Amazon is giving you that space because it wants to know what your book is about, so use it!

I'm not going to talk all day about this (I swear!). Suffice it to say that in Amazon's world, the subtitle is mostly used for marketing purposes, and this field is too often overlooked by authors who think that the subtitle has to actually appear on the book cover. That is not correct.

Here are some examples of the subtitle field being used this way. This person is doing a good job with their subtitle. Notice that the subtitle actually does not appear on the cover of the book:

Awesome Jokes That Every 6 Year Old Should Know!: Bucketloads of rib ticklers, tongue twisters and side splitters
Paperback – Illustrated, March 30, 2018
by Mat Waugh ˅ (Author), Yurko Rymar (Illustrator)
★ ★ ★ ★ ☆ ˅   7,033 ratings
Part of: Awesome Jokes for Kids (9 books)

See all formats and editions

Kindle	Paperback
$0.00 kindleunlimited	$5.99 prime
Read with Kindle Unlimited to also enjoy access to over 1 million more titles $2.99 to buy	58 Used from $0.84 17 New from $5.99

Nice! This person has used the subtitle field to include some additional descriptive adjectives that will help people find his book.

· · ·

Here's an example of what not to do:

Composition Notebook Wide Ruled
Flowers Pattern: Cute Composition
Notebook Wide Ruled Flowers Pattern,
Composition Notebook Vintage Flowers,
Flower ... for Girls, 200 7.5x9.25 Wide
Ruled Pages Paperback – July 18, 2021

by   ⌄ (Author)

★ ★ ★ ★ ☆ ·   2 ratings

See all formats and editions

Paperback
$7.43 - prime

1 New from $7.43

Yeah, no. Customers don't like this kind of thing, Amazon doesn't like it, and it looks silly. I believe it is only a matter of time before Amazon will audit the entire marketplace and penalize authors and publishers who have created these Franken-listings.

With that in mind, put something descriptive (that hopefully incorporates your keywords but is not spammy in any way) into the subtitle field! My overall point with this section was to inform you that you can use the subtitle field for keyword purposes and that the text from that field need not appear on the book cover. The more you know!

I will stop right here and say something super important, which I will intermittently bold to get your attention rather than shouting it in all caps because I'm sure you're already sick of that: **once your book is officially published** and "**Live**," you will **not** be able to make changes to the **Title, Subtitle, Author, Trim Size, Edition Number,** or **Print Options** fields. These fields will be **locked** and permanently associated with the book's ISBN.

. . .

For this reason, I recommend keeping your book in "Draft" mode until you have checked and double-checked it ad infinitum.

Next we have the "Series" field, which is one of the things that can be added later. This is optional and you can skip it if this is the first book you're publishing. If by some chance you happen to have all of your series information ready, go ahead and fill this out now.

Series   If your book is part of a series, add series details so readers can easily find the titles on a single detail page. (Optional) Learn more
Add your title to an existing series or create a new one. Linked formats for this title will be automatically added to the series once setup is complete.

Add series details

Edition Number: This is the field you fill in if you are publishing a totally new version of an already-published book. If your book has never been published, you can skip this field.

Edition Number   You can provide an edition number if this title is a new edition of an existing book. What counts as a new edition?

Edition number (Optional)

Basically, if this book has ever been published before (either by you or by another publisher), you'll need to let people know that by giving it the edition number of whatever edition it is. Also, this goes without saying, but if this is a later edition of a book that used to be with a publisher, you'll need to make 100% sure that you have the rights to this book. If you have had a book out with a publisher and they reverted your rights, you would have that in writing.

. . .

The purpose of "edition numbers" is to let consumers know that this is a different version of a book they might have bought before, to manage their expectations. What you don't want is someone buying your book thinking it's going to be totally brand-new, realizing it is a re-write of a book of yours they've already read, and complaining about it to Amazon. Granted, the chances of this happening are probably pretty small, but customer satisfaction is something Amazon takes really seriously, so be sure to choose that number correctly the first time.

Author	Enter the primary author or contributor. Pen names are allowed. Additional authors can be added in the Contributors field. This field cannot be changed after your book is published. Learn more about authorship.
	Primary Author or Contributor
	Prefix / First name / Middle name / Last name / Suffix

Contributors	If others contributed to your book, you can add them and they'll be listed on the Amazon product detail page. For multiple authors, they'll appear in the same sequence as you add them below.
	Contributors (Optional)
	Author ˅ / Prefix / First name / Middle nar / Last name / Suffix / Remove
	Add Another

Next we have the "Author" and "Contributors" sections, which are mostly self-explanatory.

Author Name

This is where you're going to put your author name (obviously). Be sure to settle on a version of your name that a) you're going to use consistently on this book and all future books you self-publish, and b) has the EXACT SAME author name as any other book you've already published on Amazon. This point concerns your Amazon Author Central page, which you want as consistent as possible in case you have to have Amazon customer service merge them at some point. This will be much harder if you've been using a bunch of different versions of your name (like, one with a middle name, one with just a middle initial, one with a hyphenated last name, and so on).

Yes, this seems like explanation overkill, but I am trying to save you time and frustration in the future. I recently had to put in a request for Amazon to merge two author pages they had created for me, and they both had the exact same spelling of my name. Weird stuff happens in the Amazon system all the time, and the easier you make it for them to fix it, the easier your life will be.

A Note About Pen Names

In case you're curious, you can totally publish under as many pen names as you want using this same KDP account. You do not need a different KDP account for each pen name, and (as I mentioned very emphatically previously), you are not allowed to have more than one KDP account, so all of your publishing (under your own name and any pen names you want to publish as) are going to be contained in this same account and on this same bookshelf. That is to say, if you are going to use a pen name, that is perfectly fine, and in fact, if one of your pen names takes off, you can blow out the "Amazon Author Central" presence for that name. Do not use a pen name like "O.K. Rowling" or you will almost certainly receive a rejection notice and be forced to change it to something else. Amazon is not amused by those kinds of shenanigans.

Also, in case you are considering doing "Publishing Company as Pen Name," I'll just let you know that Amazon is cracking down on this kind of thing (mostly because spammers are always attempting to fill Amazon with crap), so they might reject you depending on what words you're trying to use in the "First Name" and "Last Name" fields.

I'm not saying this is fair or that your company is not actually called "Million Dollar Books," but you should prepare yourself for the fact that Amazon will probably reject that as a pen name.

Contributor Name

. . .

This is where you'll put co-authors, editors, illustrators, photographers, translators, and people who contributed things like an introduction, a preface, or some other piece of writing to your book. For some weird reason, this field can be updated at any time, so if you're unsure, leave it blank and add people in later.

Next, go grab the amazing book description you wrote in Chapter 6 and copy/paste it into the "description field." If you didn't do that exercise, it's still fine to do it now, but do not leave this section blank!

You're so lucky to be publishing your book now! Amazon has updated this field to make it more like a word processing document, allowing you to make words bold, italicized, and underlined. You used to have to hand-code all of this, believe it or not! You can also add bullet points and numbered lists and make your text smaller. I recommend bolding certain words you want to emphasize, just to catch the customer's eye.

Publishing Rights

Assuming that you are the original author/ creator of the content you are uploading, check the "I own the copyright and I hold necessary publishing rights" button. I cannot caution you strongly enough against publishing "works of public domain," as this is a great way to get your account terminated. In other words (and this is just my opinion, you can feel free to disagree)— if you didn't write or create this book, you should probably not be publishing it. Not worth the risk!

Primary Audience

This section is new as of 2023 (this is why you need the electronic version of this book, with the updates! Go over to https://loricul well.com/htsp to get that!). In this section, Amazon is trying to get you to say whether the book has sexually explicit content and to (optionally) say what the reading age range is. I think it's weird that they put these questions in the same section, and I don't think this change is going to stick. My opinion!

The first "yes or no" choice in this section is asking you whether your book could be considered "sexually explicit," which they have recently changed from "adult." To clarify, by "sexually explicit," Amazon means things like erotica and sexual situations or images, not swear words. This mostly applies to fiction, but if your book has anything in it that is inappropriate for children under 18, you'll want to indicate that here so they know to exclude it from the children's sections. Do not lie about this! Amazon takes this kind of thing seriously! You probably know if you need to check that box, so if you do, go ahead and check it!

· · ·

The (strangely placed) "Reading Age" section is mostly for children's books, so go ahead and indicate the minimum and maximum ages your book might be appropriate for. There is an 18+ option in both drop-downs if you want to be incredibly thorough. This section is optional and I don't think it makes a difference unless you've written a children's book that could benefit from the reader age classification.

Categories

Okay, you've reached the "categories" section, which also has some questions about low-content and large print books. You probably are not publishing low-content or large print books, but even if you are (in which case you should check one of the appropriate boxes), you'll need to pick some categories. If you are now wondering what "low-content books" are, I wrote a whole other book about that subject, which you can find linked at the end of this book or at https://loriculwell.com.

Categories   Choose up to three categories that describe your book. Note: You must select your primary marketplace and audience first.
                    What are categories? ˅

                    Choose categories

                    Does your book classify as any of these types? Choose all that apply.
                    ☐ Low-content book (e.g. journals, notebooks, and planners) What's a low-content book? ˅
                    ☐ Large-print book (content is 16-point font size or greater) What's a large-print book? ˅

Pull out your category research! We're going in! Amazon is going to give you lists of categories to choose from, which looks like this:

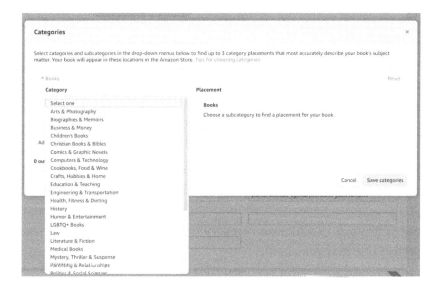

They want you to pick "up to three" categories, which means PICK THREE. That's three opportunities for your book to reach your audience.

Because you did all that research in Chapter 5, you'll immediately recognize that this is a completely different category list than the one that Amazon uses.

You are correct, and that is very observant of you! What you see here is a list of BISAC categories, which I touched on briefly when I mentioned that Amazon had exponentially improved upon this system with their 16,000+ "Browse Categories". Right now, they are going to force you to put your book into something more traditional.

In case you're curious (and why wouldn't you be, really?), BISAC stands for Book Industry Standards and Communications, and this is the list of categories/codes THEY use to classify their books. This system is a holdover from the old-school publishing industry and is still used by libraries, bookstores, and retailers. This universally agreed-upon categorization system is how bookstores and libraries know what to order and what shelves to put books on.

I have seen rare occasions where the category you chose during your research is represented in this list, but for the most part, you're going to have to sift through these old BISAC categories and put your book in whatever category of theirs that is closest to the perfect one that you chose.

What's your best next move?

The way to proceed here is to go along with what Amazon is trying to do, just to demonstrate that your book indeed fits into one of these categories and that you are following their rules. Hunt through these BISAC categories until you find two that approximate what you have on your category research list, just so you can fill these three slots and move on.

As I mentioned in the "Category Research" section, PLEASE do not freeze up and stick your book into the dreaded wasteland that is the "Uncategorized" category. That gives Amazon absolutely nothing to go on when it tries to put your book into its system (to be able to show it to potential customers later).

· · ·

Back to the BISAC. If you did your research and you have your heart set on getting your book into one of these great Amazon Browse Categories:

Best Sellers Rank: #203,406 in Books (See Top 100 in Books)
    #216 in Journalism Writing Reference (Books)
    #882 in Essays (Books)
    #4,083 in U.S. State & Local History
Customer Reviews: ☆☆☆☆☆ ˅   81 ratings

You will certainly be frustrated when you learn that, in fact, neither "Journalism Writing Reference" nor "Essays" are BISAC choices. It seems dumb and counter-intuitive that Amazon wouldn't just let you put your damn book into their system where it belongs.

Patience! You only have to do this BISAC thing once, but you have to actually play along because you need BISAC categories that are the best approximations of the Amazon Browse Categories that you're going to want, just to point Amazon in the right direction.

Next, get out the list of Browse Categories and make sure they are represented in the seven keyword boxes. If you've already filled up most of the space in those seven boxes (because I yelled about it in the last section), that's totally fine. Just make sure you have some of the same words in there. I'm sure you noticed this, but Browse Categories are mostly keywords and key phrases, so this should not be hard to do.

. . .

The combination of these two things (BISAC selection and putting the names of the Browse Categories you want into the keyword slots) will signal Amazon to start the process of putting your book where you want it. That way you can get through this upload process with some confidence.

The Seven Keyword Boxes

Here we are! Arguably the most important part of the upload interface. This is another "Catch 22" section. While Amazon is going to treat what you put in here like the writing on the Holy Grail, they do not do a great job of actually telling you this with their explanation of what goes into these all-important boxes, which is why I'm here.

These are the boxes I'm talking about, just to give you an example if you haven't logged in and tried to upload your book yet:

Here's the deal: Amazon is kind of setting you up for failure with their instructions. They SAY "choose up to 7 keywords," but the reality of what is happening behind the scenes with these boxes is that each one of them will hold UP TO FIFTY CHARACTERS and these are the primary pieces of information Amazon uses to not only rank your book for customer searches, but to put your book into their "Browse Categories" system.

Um, that would fall under "nice to know," right?

. . .

Let me repeat— FILL UP ALL THE SPACE IN THESE BOXES.

To have enough words to fill up all of this space, you will need to go back and refer to the "Keyword Research" and "Category Research" exercises in Chapters 4 and 5, respectively. Go get those lists and put those words into these boxes right now.

Amazon is going to combine all of these keywords into key phrases to deliver your book to people who are searching for it and to put it into the right categories in their own system. As you saw in the example from my website book, I filled up each and every iota of space in my seven keyword boxes, and that book is now ranking for almost 400 keywords/ key phrases. Magic!

For your reference, here is a good use of the seven keyword boxes. This is what I would do with the keyword boxes for someone who was doing a guided workbook on meditation and mindfulness. All of these words will be combined into an infinite amount of combinations, and this person's book will start appearing for those (as well as being put into the right browse categories for its genre).

Keywords	Choose up to 7 keywords that describe your book. How do I choose keywords?	
	Your Keywords (Optional)	
	self help meditation book mindfulness workbook	guide depression inspirational motivational
	stress anxiety breathing exercises peace daily	mental health education awakening wisdom
	care non fiction spiritual beginner beginning	easy simple schedule personal development
	gift Christmas birthday mom woman man student	

That's it for keywords!

Publication Date

If you're publishing a book for the very first time, you can leave this field blank. If this is an edition, just fill in the date when the book was first published.

Publication Date | The publication date tells readers when the book was originally published. If your book has not been published before, select the first option.

○ Publication date and release date are the same

○ My book was previously published

Release Date

This is another new feature that allows you to either release your book for sale as soon as you hit "publish" or (for some kinds of book) pre-schedule the release for a date sometime in the future. You'll probably use the "release my book for sale now" option.

Release Date | Choose when to make your book available on Amazon. Learn more about release date options

⦿ Release my book for sale now
After you submit for publication, it can take up to 72 hours to go live. During this time, edits cannot be made to your book. Learn more about release timelines

○ Schedule my book's release

In case you're curious, the "schedule my book's release" option is not a true "pre-order" feature, meaning your book's listing will not appear (and be available for sale) until the date you set in the schedule for it to be released. I'm not sure why you would use this feature, but if you feel like pre-scheduling your book is exactly what you need, go ahead and try it!

Ok, so— that chapter was jam-packed, and you're probably going to have to go over it a couple of times to make sure you've got everything exactly the way you want it. Remember, this is just your "first pass" at inputting all of your book's information, and as long as you don't hit "Publish," you can still change anything (or every-thing). Be sure to hit "Save as Draft" at the bottom to make sure all of your work is saved.

Great job! You could just about write your own book about self-publishing with all the knowledge you have gained thus far!

12

PAPERBACK CONTENT

Wow! That first section of the upload was a lot. You entered all of your book details (like your title, subtitle, and description), filled in your keywords, and chose your BISAC categories. Once you hit "Save and Continue," that felt like kind of a big accomplishment, right?

Great job. You are now about one-third of the way through the process of self-publishing the paperback edition of your book.

Wait... what?! Come on!

I'm kidding (sort of). Yes, this process is weirdly time-consuming, but it only takes this long the first time (I promise!). I'm trying to familiarize you with every bit of the process and answer all of the questions you might have so it'll be easier and won't take as long the next time around.

. . .

And with that, let's start from the top of the "Paperback Content" section, which is where Amazon is going to either want you to provide an ISBN (International Standard Book Number) or use one of their free ones.— This option will not be available to you if you are publishing a "low-content" book like a notebook, planner, or journal, because those types of books do not need ISBNS as of 2023.

ISBN Question(s)

You may have wondered, what is an ISBN? What do I need it for? How do I get one?

So many questions! Let's jump in. ISBN is an identifier for your book which indicates the title, author, trim size, and print options. ISBNs apply only to physical (i.e., paperback and hardcover) editions of the book, and not ebooks. Therefore, your paperback and hardcover editions will each need their own ISBN.

Print ISBN   To comply with industry standards, all paperbacks are required to have a unique ISBN. What is an ISBN? –

⊙ Get a free KDP ISBN

        Assign me a free KDP ISBN

○ Use my own ISBN

The question is, are you going to use Amazon's free ISBN, or are you going to buy an independent ISBN and use that one?

I have tried this both ways, and while I think you're probably fine using Amazon's free ISBN (especially for your very first book), the industry best-practice answer is always going to be to buy and own your ISBN yourself, so that you're not subject to the whims of Amazon and KDP. Remember, Amazon controls your account, and your use of their platform is subject to their terms of service. That means they can take your account away at any time for any reason, and all of their free ISBNs will go with it.

Here are some things to think about when you're trying to decide whether to use Amazon's free ISBN for your book or bring in one that you've paid for:

1. If you use Amazon's free ISBN, your book will appear as "Independently Published," so if you want to put the book out through your own company or brand, you will need to buy your own ISBN. This fact alone is a deal-breaker for some people, so if that's you, go over to www.bowker.org and buy a block of ISBNs right now.

2. You will not be able to publish that book anywhere else using Amazon's free ISBN. If you go to publish it somewhere else (like through Ingram), you will need to use their free ISBN, or bring in one that you bought. For continuity's sake, some authors decide they want to use the same ISBN for all platforms, so they buy it.

. . .

Some countries will give you an ISBN for free (Canada does this and I'm jealous), but in the United States, if you want to buy an ISBN, you will need to go through an ISBN agency, the best known of which is Bowker.

Like most things, ISBNs are cheaper if you buy them in bulk (in the publishing industry, this is known as a "block," so if you know you're going to publish a bunch of books, go ahead and buy a block. Bowker's bestselling block is $295 for ten ISBNs (whereas if you try to buy just one, it's $125).

Here's where to go to buy ISBNs: https://www.myidentifiers.-com/identify-protect-your-book/isbn/buy-isbn

On the KDP-setup end, the only difference is that you'll enter one of the ISBNs you bought into the ISBN field, plus you'll need to have your designer add the ISBN onto the cover prior to uploading.

Here's the bottom line. Buying your ISBN is the "best practice" and "industry standard" way to go, and if you have the budget, I say go ahead and do it that way. That said, probably 80% of authors I have worked with just use Amazon's free ISBN, so if you are trying to save money and just get your book out there, you are probably fine using the free one, then paying for one later if you find you want that.

Right now, you're like, Wow! That section went on for so much longer than I thought it could, but thanks. That was informative.

· · ·

Moving on!

Print Options

This is when you'll need to enter all of the print options for your book so that they exactly match what you specified back in the "Cover Design" section. If you don't enter everything exactly the same, there is a chance your cover will be the wrong size, and that is the thing you don't want.

Ink and Paper Type

Since we're operating on the assumption that this is a standard book (like a novel or a non-fiction book), I would recommend sticking with the standard default of "black & white interior with white paper." As I mentioned in the "Cover Design" section, cream paper looks nice, but it can limit your distribution options and makes your book a little bit thicker, so I don't usually use it.

I cover this more extensively in the Q&A section if you have more questions about color interior options. However, for our purposes here, I will drop the two most common questions I hear about color interior printing.

1. Any color in the book at all makes it "color interior." Therefore, if even one thing is in color, the whole book counts as color. This increases the cost of printing the book exponentially,— making it prohibitively expensive to buy. However...

. . .

2. ...you can always make two different versions of your book, one in black and white and one in color. If it's important to you to have that color interior version you had always envisioned, but still want a cost-effective black-and-white version as well, this is a good way to go.

Trim Size

This is the size you decided on in the prep section and formatted your book to fit. Remember? How upset would you have been if I hadn't told you this and you got to this screen with your 8.5 X 11 Word doc?

Actually, this isn't when you would have gotten upset. You would have gotten upset when you chose 6 X 9 as the trim size you wanted your book to be, then tried to upload that 8.5 x 11 doc into it. That right there is the moment I see a lot of frustrated people posting up about in publishing-related Facebook groups. (This is also when I get the call that an author is just about to give up on the whole process and now wants to hire me to walk them through the rest of it.)

I'm telling you, Amazon is presupposing that you have knowledge of an awful lot of things before they put you into a process that is supposed to be super easy.

Most people choose 6" X 9" as the dimensions for their book, so if that's what you chose (and formatted your book to be) back in the "prep" section of this book, choose that option.

Bleed vs. No Bleed

You're most likely going to want "No Bleed." Bleed is when the interior stuff in the book (words and images) goes all the way to the edge, so that's not for a regular book. Plus, once you pick "Bleed" you can only upload a pdf, and I'm guessing most of you will try this first with a word processing document. No shame! That's how I started!

Paperback Cover Finish: Matte vs. Glossy

Go over to your bookshelf right now and pick up a book that is appropriate to your genre and target demographic. Now check the finish on the cover. Matte is the flat finish, and glossy is the shiny one. I would say most of the books out there are probably glossy, but matte gives it more of a high-end, fancy look. Matte does show fingerprints, though, so if your book is going to be "handled" a lot, go with glossy. Make a note of all of these choices, because you'll need to duplicate them in the "Hardcover Upload" section.

Great job! You've now told Amazon exactly how to print your book. Your next step is going to be uploading your interior.

Manuscript Upload

Now is your first "moment of truth" in this process. Take your formatted book and upload it into the backend of the KDP system. Click the yellow "Upload paperback manuscript" button, find your finalized interior, and upload it (it'll take a second).

Next, let's move on to the "Book Cover" upload interface.

Cover Upload

Since I'm assuming you took my advice and either had a professional graphic designer make your cover or you made one yourself because you're a graphic designer, I will advise you to skip over the dreaded "Cover Creator" option (see my rant about that in the back of this book) and select "Upload a cover you already have (print-ready PDF only)."

Next, click the yellow "Upload your cover file" button, then locate the file with your finalized, print-ready cover (that you got from your designer) and upload that into the system.

DO NOT check the box that says "includes a barcode" unless you bought your own ISBN and had your designer put the barcode on the cover.

The A.I. Question

• • •

Here's another new addition to the KDP self-publishing universe:- a question about how authors and publishers are using artificial intelligence (A.I.) to help with the creation of their books.– If you choose the "Yes" button, you will then need to respond to a series of prompts indicating to what extent you have used A.I, how much editing you have done, and what programs you have used to help with your words (specifically writing and translation) and your images.

The addition of this box initially caused a wave of panic in the self-publishing industry, but the general consensus now seems to be that Amazon is just collecting information, and that they wouldn't be asking if they didn't allow A.I. at all.

In case you're curious, here is their entire (so far) policy on A.I.-generated content, which you can also find linked right here:— https://kdp.amazon.com/en_US/help/topic/G200672390

Artificial intelligence (AI) content (text, images, or translations)

We require you to inform us of AI-generated content (text, images, or translations) when you publish a new book or make edits to and republish an existing book through KDP. AI-generated images include cover and interior images and artwork. You are not required to disclose AI-assisted content. We distinguish between **AI-generated** *and* **AI-assisted** *content as follows:*

- **AI-generated:** *We define AI-generated content as text, images, or translations created by an AI-based tool. If you used an AI-based tool to create the actual content (whether text, images, or translations), it is considered "AI-generated," even if you applied substantial edits afterwards.*
- **AI-assisted:** *If you created the content yourself, and used AI-based tools to edit, refine, error-check, or otherwise improve that content (whether text or images) then it is considered "AI-assisted" and not "AI-generated." Similarly, if you used an AI-based tool to brainstorm and generate ideas, but ultimately created the text or images yourself, this is also considered "AI-assisted" and not "AI-generated." It is not necessary to inform us of the use of such tools or processes.*

You are responsible for verifying that all AI-generated and/or AI-assisted content adheres to all content guidelines, including by complying with all applicable intellectual property rights.

Book Preview

This is it! You are about to see a preview of how your book will look in print! With all the components in place, Amazon will have you hit the "Launch Previewer" button, so it can generate a print preview for you to view and approve.

Note: for whatever reason, the "Print Previewer" takes forever. No, your computer is not broken, and there is nothing wrong with your manuscript. It sometimes just takes a really long time to render the entire book into "previewable" form (even more so if you have a slow internet connection). Just hang out, and eventually the "Print Previewer" will appear.

If your manuscript and cover have errors (meaning something is too small, too large, or formatted incorrectly), you will see an error message on the left-hand side of your screen. You will not be given the option to approve the book and move on to the next screen until you solve whatever problem the Quality Check has found, and you'll need to make these changes to your book's original manuscript file and re-save it. After that, you'll need to go back, re-upload, and see if the changes you made have satisfied the quality check.

If the problem turns out to be with your cover, you'll need to have your designer make the changes (and this is why I advised you earlier not to finalize your cover until you have passed the upload process).

· · ·

This whole thing might take a few tries, so don't get frustrated! This is a normal part of the process. If your manuscript and cover are both perfectly sized and the Quality Check finds no errors, you will not see any error messages on the left-hand side, and the "Approve" button will be yellow, meaning you theoretically could approve the manuscript, set the pricing and distribution, and make the book live right now.

You will want to do this because you are excited, and you're human, and you want to publish your book already. But! This is another one of those moments where I will strongly recommend (to the point of all caps) that you DO NOT SKIP THE PREVIEW AND RUSH INTO PUBLISHING.

No, in fact, this is the point where I recommend to all of my author clients that they go through the entire book page by page at least one time all the way through, just to make sure everything is where you put it. By that, I mean headings, page numbers, images, dedications, and anything else that might be inside that book.

I get it. You really want to get your book out there! You're so close, and going through your entire book page by page sounds like it is going to take forever. But I'm begging you, take the time to go through it at least once, because this is that moment. If you rush through this part and miss something you could have fixed (like chapter headings being off or an image being in the wrong place) and you get a one-star review based on quality, you are going to be filled with regret.

·   ·   ·

You will most likely repeat this cycle a couple of times, just making little tweaks until the book is exactly the way you want it. You can update the manuscript anytime (even after the book is published), but you really want to make sure that it is as perfect as it can be before you hit "Publish" on it.

If the book (meaning cover and interior) has passed not only Amazon's Quality Check but your own page-by-page read-through, go ahead and hit "Approve," and you'll be done with this section. Amazon will then give you a "Summary" at the bottom of the screen, indicating how much it will cost to print your book.

Whew! Great job! You're done with this section! So you know, that was the heaviest lifting you'll ever have to do, and it'll all be smooth sailing from here on out. Yay!

13
PAPERBACK RIGHTS AND PRICING

You made it! You're on the very last screen of the upload! You've run the gauntlet of uploading your manuscript and cover, and you've gone through the entire manuscript page by page, made the necessary corrections, and re-uploaded. You've even passed the dreaded "Quality Control" check.

You are now confident in the quality of the book itself, so you just need to make a couple more decisions before you release it out into the wild (so to speak).

The first one is: where will my book be distributed? You will need to designate the territories where your book will be sold to answer that question.

Territories

If you wrote the book yourself and want it distributed worldwide, you will leave this set to "All territories (worldwide rights)."

If you have some issue where you can't distribute in certain countries, select the "Individual territories" option. This will give you (at last count) 249 territories that you can select individually.

The only issues I have ever heard of where someone has needed the "Individual territories" option were things like:

1. An author gets a book back from a publisher who has given them back the rights to re-release it, but the book rights have already been sold to other countries, which would limit their ability to select "all," because then they would be competing against the foreign distributors.

2. An author is somehow not able to distribute to a certain territory because of copyright issues (e.g., if you wrote a book that contained quotes from the King James Version of the Bible, which

is not in the public domain in the United Kingdom). If you have any doubts about this, definitely do some more due diligence and/or consult an attorney. If you were in this situation, you would probably know it.

Pricing

How much should your book cost? That is a question only you can answer (with a tiny bit of help from Amazon). Luckily, pricing can be changed after you publish the book, but I want you to feel as confident as possible when you hit "Publish," and knowledge is power!

The "pricing" screen looks like this:

Pricing, royalty, and distribution	Enter the list price you'd like to sell your book for. You can also make your book available to bookstores and other distributors, reaching readers beyond Amazon. This is optional and limited to certain marketplaces. How does pricing and royalties work?

Marketplace	List Price	Printing	Amazon Rate	Royalty	Expanded Distribution Rate	Royalty
Amazon.com	$ USD Min $4.30, Max $250.00. All marketplaces are based on this price		60%	–	40%	–

Amazon will show your minimum price underneath the pricing box, so that's where you'll start. That's all the guidance on pricing they will give you, since they are already making their money on the printing side. In other words, they don't care if you price your book at the "Minimum Price" they suggest, even though that will mean you make almost no royalties. We got into the publishing game not only to be published authors but also to pay for stuff, so let's get you some money for your hard work.

· · ·

First, we need to get a feel for the average price of books in your genre and category. Pull out your competitive analysis (and no, I will never stop with this, especially not after it has been so super useful at so many times in this process!) and take a look at the prices of your top five-to-ten competitive books. You'll need to price your book at a rate that makes your book competitive with the competition while still making you a profit. Paperbacks, ebooks, and hardcovers all have different fee structures on the Amazon side, and you set the price of each version independently. I would aim to make at least $2 in profit per book, so start there and go up as your market allows. You also might want to set your price kind of low in the beginning just to get the momentum going.

Amazon will then calculate your book's price in all of the international marketplaces where it will be offered. You are about to be an internationally published author!

If you're curious about what is going on with the "expanded distribution" check box, that's where Amazon will offer your book to its list of distributors, which includes a lot of bookstores and libraries. "Hey, that's awesome," you think to yourself, and you're right. But just so you know, they're not going to tell you which distributors are on their list, whether they are actually pitching your book to them, and which ones have accepted it. How very Amazon of them! If you decide to check this box, it's best to think of your "expanded distribution" money, which will arrive in one big chunk once a month, as a delightful bonus.

If you want to control more about this "expanded distribution' situation, you're better off not checking this box and putting your book in at IngramSpark, which I will cover in Chapter 17 (Going Wide: Alternate Distribution). Make a note of that for the future (when the dust has settled on this launch and you have your wits about you again).

Request a Proof Copy

Here I am again, shouting in all caps: DO NOT SKIP THIS STEP!

I feel like this process is not made clear enough in the KDP interface, so I am going to lay it out step by step, just for your reference.

Before you hit the publish button, I *strongly* recommend that you take the time to order a physical proof copy from Amazon, so you can hold your book in your hands before you officially send it out into the world. After all the work you've put into this process, the last thing you want is for there to be some problem with the manuscript that you didn't catch in the print preview and for someone to leave you a one-star review based on that problem. So you're aware, Amazon will absolutely not take down reviews like that, even if you fix the errors, so you need to make sure your book is absolutely perfect before you make it live, and this is your last chance to do that. Do not take the risk of having that book live on the Amazon marketplace for ONE MINUTE until you have held the book in your hands and looked through the entire thing.

THIS IS MY ALL CAPS WARNING TO YOU! I have made this mistake, and it is absolutely heartbreaking when it happens. It will take the wind out of your sails, make you want to never write another word, and also make you want to kick yourself. All at the same time! (Yes, it is possible to feel all these things at once. I did, while also crying in my car.)

·   ·   ·

Now that I've convinced you that you absolutely must order a proof, here is exactly how to do it. I'm going to walk you through the "proof ordering" process of the hardcover version of my book "Funny You Should Ask: How to Make a Website," which I screen-shotted just for you.

Here I am at the very end of my book's upload process (pricing, royalties, and distribution). Amazon puts the "Order a Proof" option in a place where you can blink and miss it, and sadly, if you hit the "Publish" button (which you are excited to do!), your book will be live and you will have skipped this step.

This is the link you're looking for. Wow! That is super tiny!

Why do they make the "Request printed proofs" link so small and unobtrusive?! Who knows? Anyway, click it, and it will take you to a page that looks like this:

Choose the quantity (I always just get one, but you may want more), then choose the marketplace where you want to buy the book (U.S., Europe, etc.).

In case you didn't read the fine print, which I didn't for years, this is a *proof* copy, not an author copy. This means it will have a "Not for Resale" watermark on the cover and the barcode. Do not be alarmed—this is just written on there to keep you from reselling the proof copy, but it will not be printed on the actual copies once the book goes live.

. . .

Let's all pause now to acknowledge the rich irony of the fact that Amazon is writing something on the proof copy of the book, which is supposed to be the closest thing we have to a perfect copy before it goes to print. Um, okay. That's not confusing.

Back at the pricing screen, you're obviously not going to be hitting that "Publish Your Book" button until the proof arrives and you see it for yourself, so you'll need to choose the "Save as Draft" option and leave the book sitting in your bookshelf unpublished.

Great progress! Once you have the book in your hands and have reviewed it, you will be ready to move forward with the publishing process.

Here are a couple of things you can do while you're waiting:

1. Upload your ebook

2. Upload your Hardcover

3. Verify that your book cover looks amazing in thumbnail form (and make corrections if it doesn't)

4. Reach out to early reviewers who are reading your manuscript to make sure they are ready to leave reviews once your book has officially launched

. . .

5. Send an email to your list, just telling them where you are in the process and talking to them about how excited you are that your book is finally coming out.

6. Plan the book launch party you are about to throw for yourself. What is your favorite kind of cake?

When the proof copy arrives and you're satisfied with it, log back in, double-check all the information in each of the three tabs (Details, Content, Pricing/Distribution), then—and only then!—can you click the yellow "Publish" button.

Wow! You did it! The big moment at last! Take a victory lap and high-five yourself for doing such an awesome job.

Just so you're aware, it's going to take a few days for Amazon to review and approve your book. This is totally normal and does not mean Amazon has anything against you or your writing.

If Amazon finds any problems with your book, you will be notified via email. Some of the most common problems are things like using a pen name they think is spammy, repeating your keywords too many times in your title or subtitle, or using content that is "freely available on the internet." But we know none of those scenarios will apply to you since I mentioned all of them as examples. Right? Right!

. . .

In about 24 to 48 hours, you will be notified that your book is approved and is for sale! More high-fives and victory laps!

14

THE HARDCOVER UPLOAD

I'm totally envious of your self-publishing journey right now, because Amazon recently rolled out hardcovers as an option for books self-published through KDP. This was something previously unheard of that the whole self-publishing community has been waiting on for about as long as we've been publishing books, and it finally launched in 2021! As a self-publishing nerd, please believe me when I tell you that this was one of the most exciting things to happen in all of 2021 and that indie authors were talking about it all year.

Even if you don't usually buy a hardcover version of books, don't skip this step! Having a hardcover version of your book is not just awesomely legitimizing and makes you feel as much like a traditionally published author as a self-published person has honestly ever been able to. It's also a great additional revenue stream that you can set up without too much additional effort. Yes, hardcovers do cost more (a lot more, actually, and we'll get to that later), but some people just prefer them, so it's smart to give them that option, especially since the whole process is so easy.

Let's jump in and get the hardcover version of your book submitted while we're waiting for the paperback to go live!

This chapter is going to seem comically short (especially compared to the last few mini-marathons I just put you through) because the hardcover process essentially repeats the paperback process (right down to using the exact same interior file you used for the paperback, provided you took my advice and chose one of the five trim sizes that can exist as both paperback and hardcover), just with a slightly differently sized cover and a higher price.

I recommend doing this either right after you order the paperback proof of your book or after you hit the publish button on your paperback and you're waiting for it to be approved. You'll want the whole process you just went through with the paperback to be fresh in your mind, and also, you'll get a kick out of how much of that paperback work you get to re-purpose. You basically yield two books for the price of one, effort-wise.

In fact, Amazon KDP wants you to add a hardcover version of your book so much they actually help you out by filling out the whole "Hardcover Details" section for you! This is great, but so you're aware, it's also a potential "gotcha" moment. In order to ensure the hardcover version of your book is linked to the paperback and the ebook, you need to select the "+Create Hardcover" button BELOW YOUR EXISTING PAPERBACK.

+ Create Kindle eBook

Link existing Kindle eBook

Why offer multiple formats? ⌄

Paperback

LIVE ⌄

View on Amazon ⌄

PAPERBACK ACTIONS

Order author copies   ...

+ Create hardcover

Link existing hardcover

Why offer multiple formats? ⌄

I went all-caps just now because it is super important that you click the "+Create Hardcover" button on the *existing listing for your book,* rather than getting distracted and choosing the hardcover option under "Create a New Title" at the top of the page. If you make the mistake of doing that, you're going to be lost in a morass of bureaucracy that will rival a Kafka novel when you try to join that hardcover version to the paperback listing, plus you won't get the benefit of having everything pre-filled for you, so you will lose the amazing opportunity Amazon is giving you to repurpose all the hard work you just did on the paperback!

As I mentioned above, when you click the "+ Create Hardcover" button below your paperback, you'll find that the entire first section (in this case, "Hardcover Details") is pre-filled with the same information you painstakingly added to the Paperback Details section, which is super convenient. So go ahead and click that "+Create Hardcover" button, and let's get started!

· · ·

See? Magic! One click, and BAM! the whole first section is done!

I'm using a lot of exclamation points right now because I'm trying to win you back from those terribly long "Paperback Upload" chapters. Look, I know they were arduous, but now here you are with two versions of your book for the price of one! That's huge!

With that in mind, since you spent a ton of time inputting, checking, and double-checking these details during the paperback upload, just give everything the once-over, add or fix anything you want to fine-tune for this version, and you're good to go! Be sure to add "hardcover" into the description and the keyword boxes (and take away paperback/softcover, obviously), then go ahead and hit "Save and Continue" to get yourself to the next section.

Wow! That was so quick, right? Don't you feel super productive right now?!

Seriously. Please forgive me for those last three chapters. There was no other way!

At the top of the next page, you'll assign one of Amazon's free ISBNs to the hardcover version (each printed version needs its own), or you'll use another one of your paid ISBNs for this one. Either is fine!

Everything in the "Hardcover Content" section is the exact same as it was in "Paperback Content," so refer back to that (again, quite substantial and arduous) chapter if you need to refresh your memory.

When you arrive at "Trim Size," you will notice that there are substantially fewer choices for book sizes than you had in the paperback section. As I alluded to earlier, this is the moment when I hope you took my advice and made your manuscript one of those standard sizes that can be done in both paperback and hardcover, because if you did, you're going to sail through this section as well.

The "Print Options" choices are not pre-filled for you, but it should be pretty easy to remember everything you chose for the paperback. If you followed all the standard options I recommended, your paperback book is probably 6 X 9, no bleed, white paper, and glossy finish (or something like that). Duplicate those here.

Next, you're just going to repeat the same steps that you did for the paperback upload. Click the "Upload hardcover manuscript" button, go find the interior manuscript file you used for your paperback, select it, and wait for it to upload into the system.

On the slight chance you did not take my advice to make your hardcover manuscript in one of the sizes available to both paperback and hardcover, you will now need to designate which trim size you are using, then go back to your original manuscript, resize it for one of the sizes Amazon can currently do in hardcover form (see the chart in Chapter 8), and re-format the book to fix any formatting errors created by the resizing.

. . .

Next up is the cover, the hardcover version of which you have ideally gotten from your designer. Click the "Upload your cover file" button, go find the hardcover cover (ha!) file you got from your designer, select it, and wait for it to upload into the system. DO NOT attempt to upload your paperback's cover into this hard-cover interface, or you will get a quality-check error. The cover for the hardcover is a completely different size!

In case you're curious as to why (again, are you? Probably not), Amazon's hardcover books are **case laminate**, which means the cover file needs to have a lot of extra space around the outer edges so it can be wrapped and glued onto the cover (even if the paper-back and the hardcover are the exact same size). Case laminate is where the cover is glued onto the book cover itself (rather than it being a hardcover book with a dust jacket). Despite case laminate being the cheaper hardcover option (yes, I am a book snob), these are actually decent quality, and I have been really happy with every book of mine I've started offering as hardcover.

Because you already ran the paperback upload gauntlet, I'm assuming your book is going to sail through the print preview without any quality-check errors, so you won't even need to go through the entire manuscript page by page again before hitting "Approve." Easy peasy!

Moving right along to the Hardcover Rights & Pricing section, you'll set everything the exact same as you had it for your paper-back (in terms of territories and marketplace).

· · ·

Take a deep breath, because you'll need to be calm when you get to the "pricing" section. The required pricing for the hardcover is a rude awakening for most authors, probably because we don't want to seem like we're overcharging for our books. Amazon's printing cost for hardcovers is expensive, so they are going to require you to charge an arm and a leg for your book's hardcover edition. Yes, this is silly, and yes, you have to play along. Just remind yourself that if someone is going to buy the hardcover edition of your book, they are going to be willing to pay more. Besides, this process was so easy, and this is yet another potential income stream for you, so set a price at which you make about $2 in royalties, and try not to be bothered by the fact that the hardcover version of your book is something like $16.99, even though you would like it to be less. I will tell you from personal experience that I have released hardcover versions of books and can report that even with the inflated pricing, I have made some sales!

You'll then see that sneaky little "Request printed proofs of this book" link at the bottom of the page. If you want to order a proof copy of the hardcover so you can look at it before it goes live, now is your one and only chance! I usually skip this step since I've gotten a proof of the paperback, but if you want to make 100% sure you like the hardcover version, order this now or forever hold your peace.

That's it! As soon as you're ready, hit the "Publish your Hardcover" button and wait for this version of your book to go live!

Come on! That totally made up for those three long paperback chapters!

. . .

Right...?

15

THE EBOOK UPLOAD

Okay, you're waiting on one or more things—the arrival of the proof copy of the paperback (and maybe the hardcover), the approval of one or both versions of the printed books, and so on. The next thing to do is upload your ebook.

Great news! Because you have put so much time and energy into research and formatting and are now such an expert due to the fact that I made you run the whole gamut of uploading your paperback first, this Kindle upload is going to be super-duper easy. Also, if you're keeping track, this is your third iteration of this book for the price of one!

As with the hardcover upload, this is the only possible "gotcha" moment of this process. In order to ensure the ebook version of your book is linked to the paperback and hardcover versions, you need to select the "+ Create Kindle eBook" button *above your existing paperback.*

That's this button right here, in case you're just joining us:

Just like that amazing moment in the hardcover upload, one click and that whole first section is DONE! You have once again repurposed countless hours of work to create another version of your book!

Note: If for some reason you are ignoring my advice to first publish your book as a paperback so none of this stuff is filled out for you, you'll still need to go back through the paperback-upload section for the blow-by-blow description of what each field means and what to put in it, because no one wants me to go over all of that again here.

· · ·

Now we're rolling, am I right? This is going to be the most satisfying of the three processes, for this one has almost instant gratification!

Go ahead and eyeball the pre-filled sections, which should look absolutely perfect, given the amount of time you put into research. The good news with the ebook is that since there is no ISBN to which to tie all the metadata, you can come back and update any of the information (including the title, subtitle, and author) at any time.

There are just a couple of differences in the ebook vs. paperback upload process, so we'll just briefly touch on those here.

Title

There is a tiny difference here that may get you hung up in Amazon's manual review process, so I will bring it up now to hopefully stop that from happening. Whereas in the paperback upload, you're only required to match the title to what's on the spine of the book, for ebooks, you'll need everything you have on the cover to appear in the title field. The reason for that is because with ebooks, there is obviously no spine. This is probably not a concern for you, but on the off chance it does apply, I am mentioning it now just as an FYI.

Pre-order

This is a cool feature that was recently added and doesn't get used enough, so I will tell you a little about it here. Pre-order gives you the opportunity to put the electronic version of your book on pre-order for up to a year in advance, which you can use to generate interest in the book. I will warn you, *be careful* with this pre-order feature if you haven't written your book yet, because if you try to push your release date back (or God forbid, miss the release date), Amazon will suspend you from the pre-order program for a year.

Here are some things I can tell you about pre-order:

—During the pre-order phase, Amazon will take orders for the book, which it will then fulfill when you release the finalized manuscript. This can be a cool thing to have, especially if you already have people asking about your book.

—Pre-order sales do count toward the book's BSR (bestseller rank), so that can be a cool way to promote the book or gauge interest in the topic

.

—During the "pre-order" timeline, Amazon will send you naggy email reminders. This will probably help your procrastination problem, but it might also give you writer's block, depending on how you respond to stress. You know yourself!

Also, here's a really, really important thing that is not made clear about pre-orders, but which would have been great to know for one of my clients to whom this happened (and for all authors who tend to wait until the very last minute when they have a deadline):

Despite being headquartered in Seattle, Amazon's clocks for KDP actually work on Greenwich Mean Time (GMT).

Maybe you can see where I'm going with this.

When your book is enrolled in the Amazon pre-order program, you assign your book a release date, and Amazon gives you an upload deadline. If by some strange chance you happen to be like every other author in the world and wait until the very last minute to put the final touches on your manuscript and submit it, be sure that you do so before midnight Greenwich Mean Time (GMT).

I'm not saying you're going to do this, but should you be the kind of author that waits until the very last moment and you do that on your release date, technically you will have missed it, and you will be suspended from using the pre-order program for one year.

Yes, you read that right. You don't even want to know how I know this.

I guess what I'm saying is, pre-order is super cool and can do a lot for your career, but it is not a feature I recommend for beginning self-published authors, especially if you're not done with your book. Don't take the risk!

. . .

I've probably scared you enough, so let's move on your Kindle ebook content.

Manuscript

Next, you're going to answer one question about Digital Rights Management, then upload your ebook manuscript (which you have prepared and saved in the folder on your desktop).

Digital Rights Management (DRM) is what's supposed to keep people from distributing your book without authorization. There are schools of thought for and against the whole concept of DRM, and I'm really agnostic about this whole concept, so I will let you Google the finer points if you find piracy concerning or want to learn more.

Theoretically, enabling DRM is supposed to stop people from distributing your book or reading it on different devices, but I frankly have never seen the problem with letting as many people read my books as possible (even for free! Honestly! Would you like a free book?). With that in mind, I have tried this DRM thing both ways and have seen absolutely no difference, so pick the one you're more comfortable with! One thing to consider is that you can't change the DRM setting after your ebook is published, so choose something you can live with and move on.

As I mentioned in the section on formatting your ebook, you need to have done the formatting to make sure your ebook has functional navigation before you upload it here. As a reminder, you need the table of contents and all the links in the book to be active and clickable, plus the book needs to look great on electronic reading devices (you're about to be able to look at your ebook in preview form, so you'll know if it will work).

I've said it before, and I'll say it again: Amazon does not format! Do all of this before you upload!

Kindle ebook Cover

Next up is the cover upload. Grab the Kindle version of the cover you got from your designer (or made yourself) and upload it here. If you're just getting to this now, here are some things you need to know:

—You'll just need the front cover for the ebook version.

—The image for your Kindle eBook cover will need to be a .tiff or a .jpeg. Amazon doesn't like pngs, and I can't really tell you why.

—Ideal dimensions for your cover file is 2560 x 1600 (2560 pixels high x 1600 pixels wide).

—Cover file must be at least 1000 x 625 (1000 pixels high x 625 pixels wide).

. . .

Click the "Upload your cover file" button, find the cover, and upload it. You're almost done!

Kindle ebook Preview

Okay, here we go! Click the "Launch Previewer" button to see how your ebook will look on people's devices.

(Remember, this is a work in progress! Don't get too upset if it doesn't look perfect, because you can always go back and fix it using the additional resources in Chapter 10)

Hopefully you will love the way it looks, and you can easily move on from here. If not, take a deep breath, go back to your original document and make changes, then re-upload. If you tried to do the "Basic/DIY Word Processing Document" method and that didn't work, maybe move on to Kindle Create to try to format it. If that doesn't work, consider some paid options like Atticus or Vellum. You'll get there!

Downloadable Preview Options

This is where Amazon tells you that you can download your book and look at it in the Kindle app. Give it a try if you think it will go better than with the online previewer! I have personally never been able to get this thing to work, and I'm always surprised when I go to upload a new book and find this feature is still there.

· · ·

Still, if you use it and it helps you, fantastic! Whatever gets you there!

ISBN

You don't need an ISBN for an ebook, so I wouldn't waste one (even if you are using paid ISBNs for your printed books). If you bought a block of them and you absolutely want to put it in there (because you're trying for continuity of publisher across editions), this is where to put it!

If you need a little refresher on what ISBNs are, where to get them, and whether you want free vs. paid, go back to Chapter 12 to revisit my scintillating ISBN coverage.

Once that's all done, click "Save and Continue" and you're on to the next page!

KDP Select Enrollment

I'm going to say some things here that you might find a little controversial, but hear me out. I wouldn't tell you anything without trying it first, and I have approached this issue from every single angle since the moment Amazon started offering this service years ago.

. . .

I enroll my books in KDP Select when they first launch to get that extra marketing push, but I don't leave them in there for the long term, which means they do not appear in Kindle Unlimited forever. This is also the strategy I encourage my author clients to follow.

Here are my reasons for not using KDP Select for the long term:

1. Lack of diversification. I really want authors (including myself) to get their work out there as far and wide as possible. Since paperbacks (and now hardcovers) are really Amazon's realm, that really only gives you the ebook version of your book that you can actually get better distribution on, and you do by putting it everywhere from Barnes & Noble to Baker & Tayler, from Google Play to the Apple Store.

Unless, that is, you check that little box enrolling the book in KDP Select, which prohibits you from putting it in those places. For me, that's a deal-breaker. You're self-publishing because you want to be in control of your book's distribution, so it makes zero sense to give all that power over to Amazon.

Also, let us not forget the small segment of the population that absolutely will not buy things from Amazon. Those people will never hear about your work if Amazon is the only place they can find it.

Finally—and I am loathe to even say this out loud because I am so superstitious (it's true, ask my husband!)—if by some weird fluke, Amazon decides to terminate your KDP account, that's it for your book. It is gone and it no longer exists in Amazon's universe. In that event, you'll need your other sales channels as "alternates."

I'm not saying that's ever going to happen to you (unless you are planning on taking a public domain book and republishing it, in which case it is absolutely going to happen to you), but for that reason alone, I would recommend not putting all of your eggs in Amazon's basket

2. Lack of conversion. Beyond the diversification problem (which is really number one for me), I have just not been that impressed with how my books have done when I've put them in KDP Select. Yes, they are part of Kindle Unlimited (which, if you don't know, is an Amazon-exclusive membership that lets you read ebooks for free), but I have not found the exposure my books get through that program to make up for the fact that I can't put them anywhere else on the internet. Like, maybe if Amazon was willing to actually promote your books and tell people about them in exchange for enrollment, it might be worth it, but they don't, so it's not.

3. Lack of money. Because I pay extremely close attention to reporting (see the chapter on reporting in which I talk about my love affair with KDP Champ), I can actually see people reading my books in real time.

My anecdotal experience (and you can go ahead and take this with a grain of salt) is that people *think* they want to read a book they got for free through KU, but when the rubber meets the road, they'll read about 1/3 to 1/2 of the book and then quit. You only get paid for actual pages read, and you are not going to enjoy the fractions of pennies you make even when people finish your whole book under the KU program.

But listen! I don't know everything! If you know some expert that has a whole KDP Select strategy that is going to get you a huge following or make you a million bucks, do it! I actually have heard that KDP Select works great for authors who write certain kinds of genre fiction and have a bunch of books in a series. If that is you, KDP Select is probably worth a try! Just make sure you only enroll your book for 90 days (without automatic renewal). You'll need to actually log in and uncheck the box that says "automatically re-enroll my book into KDP Select every 90 days."

Here are some things you *can* do if you put your book into KDP Select:

—Free promotion. KDP Select lets you give your book away for free for up to 5 days, every 90-day period. This is only a thing I would advise you to do if you have one of the following: 1) a really compelling call to action (and that landing page link) inside your book or 2) a bunch of other books in a series for which you're trying to get exposure. If either of these things apply to you, go ahead and put your book into KDP Select for 90 days so you can try out the free promotion. In each of these cases, you're using your book as a loss leader or lead magnet to get you readers, which is a perfectly valid strategy. Do not under any circumstances make your book free if it doesn't at least have a link to a landing page with a free offer in exchange for an email (as discussed in Chapter 7 and the free ebook). What if your book takes off and you miss out on all those potential subscribers? Just thinking about this makes me sad on your behalf.

. . .

—Kindle Countdown Deal. This is when you set your book at an enticingly low price for a limited period of time with the hope it will catch the attention of people who like buying discounted books. This is fine to try, but as I mentioned above, please either have a prominent link to that landing page/ signup or a bunch of other books you're trying to promote if you do this. I only want you to discount your work if it's going to get you something!

Please note: As I mentioned, KDP Select is an exclusive program, so if you end up taking my advice and distributing your ebook more widely, you will not be able to go back. This is why I tell people, if you're going to experiment with KDP Select, do it at the very beginning of your book's life, see if it does anything for you, and then move on.

Okay, I've talked enough about a thing you've probably never even heard of, so let's move on!

Leave your territories set to "all" unless you have a reason not to (extended discussion on this is in the section on paperback uploads, so I won't repeat it here), then set your primary market-place to wherever you expect the majority of your sales to come from.

Next up is pricing, and then your book is live! Select one of the following:

Select a royalty plan and set your Kindle eBook list prices below
○ 35%   ◉ 70%

You're like: "Huh? Who would choose a lower royalty on purpose?" I'm sure you don't want another lengthy explanation of why Amazon does things, so I will attempt to make this brief.

You're not wrong, it looks completely weird and is unnecessarily confusing. The story goes like this. Amazon wants you to charge between $2.99 and $9.99 for your ebook, and that is when they are going to give you that really good 70% royalty. If you make things difficult for them by charging too little (like 99 cents) or too much (like 99 dollars), they are only going to give you 35% royalty in exchange for that hassle.

The "99-cent book" strategy used to be a thing years ago, and you can go ahead and try it out if you have other books to promote or you're using your book as a loss-leader to try to get people onto your email list (just like the free promotion scenario I mentioned above). Generally speaking, I like authors to make at least $2 royalty per book, including ebooks, so I would advise you to avoid the 35% button like the plague (Wow! That expression suddenly became more relevant!).

My best advice on pricing is to choose the 70% button, go back to your competitive analysis from chapter 3 to see what your competitors are charging for their ebooks, and then set your price accordingly (just make sure you're making at least $2 royalty per book).

. . .

Your very last move is to decide whether you want to enable Kindle Book Lending (yes, you can do this even if you have selected the "Digital Rights Management" option). I usually just leave this set to "Allow lending for this book," but you can do whatever makes you feel comfortable.

Lastly, agree to the terms and conditions, then hit "Publish." Your book will then enter a brief review period, after which it will be live and buyable!

Congratulations! You are done with your part of the self-publishing process! You are now waiting for Amazon to approve the different versions of your book and for them all to appear on the same listing page. Give it a few days to make sure you've seen the proof copy and to make sure everything is showing up on the listing, then move on to the "What's Next?" section to start telling people about it!

For now, though, give yourself a hand! And let's shout it in all caps: YOU ARE A PUBLISHED AUTHOR!

PART 3: NOW WHAT?

Yay! Your book is live!

Now what?

So many things! This section covers getting your book out there to even more outlets and marketplaces if you want wider distribution, and starting to get your book out there, marketing-wise. I do have a whole other book on author platforms and book marketing, but I did just want to introduce the concept and give you some tips in this book as well. This is your book's "honeymoon phase" with Amazon, where they're going to show it to more people to see if it takes off, so you owe it to yourself (and your book) to do everything you can to get it some exposure!

Congratulations again. You are a published author, and that is a huge deal!

Now, let's get back to work.

16

GOING WIDE: ALTERNATE DISTRIBUTION CHANNELS

Your book is on Amazon. Fantastic! Because I am a big believer in not putting all your eggs in one basket, I will now encourage you to get on some other platforms so that your book will be distributed to a wider audience. Here are some ways to do that!

After you've gotten your book's Amazon listing situated, your next move is going to be to distribute it to other bookselling market-places throughout the internet (and the world). Once again, all of your prep work is going to really pay off here, since you already have your ebook properly formatted and saved as an ePub (as well as a properly-formatted cover), so you really just need to decide how much time (and money) you're going to give to the list of other marketplaces. (Note: if your book happens to still be in "docx" form, now is the time to revisit the discussion on proper ebook formatting in Chapter 9.)

Why do I recommend wider distribution?

On its face, you would employ a strategy of wider (meaning, outside of Amazon) distribution because you want your book to be available in as many marketplaces and to as many potential readers as possible.

That is true, but the reason I recommend this is mostly because I simply do not want you to rely exclusively on Amazon for your career success. If you don't do at least a little bit of wider distribution to get your book into some other places and, God forbid, something happens to your Amazon account, you will be left with zero streams of income. I don't want that to happen to you. Also, you put all that work into your book, and I think you should repurpose that work on as many marketplaces as possible. Trust me here—it's not that hard!

Also, I have mentioned this before, but it bears repeating: Some people do not like Amazon and will not use it. That means that if your book only exists in the world of Amazon, you are cutting yourself off from potential readers. Even if you only sell one or two books per month in other marketplaces, that's extra money and potential fans you wouldn't have had before, so I believe it's worth the setup time.

I will also throw in a quick (but related) side note on the SEO and reputation management benefits of putting your work on multiple marketplaces. It is a good idea to get your work out there on a wider scale because it is better for you and your life to have your name and book existing on multiple websites that have large digital footprints. I won't go down a reputation-management rabbit hole because that's the subject of another book (which I am currently writing), but it is always, *always* much better to have your name out there on multiple sites, so you have a decent buffer when people Google you. This becomes 100% more true if you ever do something "cancellable" and end up needing to push unfavorable Google results down.

Again, I'm not even going there right now. Suffice it to say, I think you should take your work and put it on as many marketplaces as will have you.

ebook Distribution: A Big Ol' Complicated Hot Mess

Let's talk brass tacks. If you took my advice and did not enroll in KDP Select, you are free to distribute your ebook to all of the other online platforms that are not Amazon. Sadly, there is no one-stop-shop for doing that, so I will do my best to explain what you'll need to do next.

If you *did* enroll your book in KDP Select, you will not be able to distribute it more widely until you un-enroll it and wait for the 90-day contract to expire. (If this is you, just make a note in your calendar to come back and do the rest of the distribution once 90 days are up.) Also, for reasons that are now self-evident, I will remind you not to check the auto-renewal box when it comes to anything related to Amazon (but especially with KDP Select).

. . .

In terms of wider-distribution strategy, your best practice will be to sign up with the top four alternate publishers (which I have listed below) and publish your book through each one manually. This will give you access to all of their reporting and promotional features, as well as the highest royalty rate on each. Once you're done registering individually with these sites and publishing your book on each, you will then move on to one or more aggregate publishers (don't worry, I am just about to define this term) to get your book out to even more markets (as well as libraries!).

I have to tell you all of this because I'm trying to be as thorough as possible, knowing full well that 99 out of 100 people are not going to do all (or even most) of this. For those 99 people, read on! There is a (slightly) better way!

If you are already completely over the concept of publishing in a bunch of other places and you don't really care that much about the possibility of a slightly higher royalty (plus the use of each publisher's promotional tools), you can skip to the section on aggregate publishers, because they will also distribute to these outlets.

Look, I know this is confusing. This is a big old hot mess in the indie publishing industry, and some people talk only about this. We'll get through it together. Promise.

Without further ado, here are the top four places besides Amazon to distribute your book:

Google Play Books

The Google gods are for sure not going to be excited if they ever discover that I have placed their fine "Google Play Books marketplace" on an "others" list, but let's get real: you've never heard of Google Play Books before now, am I wrong?

Google Play Books actually has 5 million digital titles for sale, so they are technically "one of the world's largest bookstores." Who knew?

Visit https://play.google.com/books/publish/u/0/ to sign up. You'll then be asked to enter your financial information so Google can pay you, and then you'll need to add your book, which will be zero problem for you after all of the work you did, both in the prep section of this book and during the Amazon upload process. I do think you should put your book in here because I am currently testing a theory that doing so actually makes your book title show up as a search result in Google. Check www.loriculwell.com or www.bookpromotion.com for more on that as the story develops.

Check back once or twice a month to see if you made any sales!

Barnes & Noble Press

https://press.barnesandnoble.com/

Yes, Barnes & Noble is still a thing! Barnes & Noble Press focuses on the United States and has about 1 million titles. If you are so inclined, open an account, become a "vendor" by entering your contact and payment info, and upload your ebook into their marketplace. Barnes & Noble will make it worth your while by giving you access to online promotional opportunities. If you are a big B&N or Nook user, this might be one of the ones you want to manage yourself!

Kobo Writing Life

https://www.kobo.com/us/en/p/writinglife

Kobo (now known as Rakuten Kobo after a recent merger with affiliate marketing giant Rakuten) has millions of readers all over the world, partly because they distribute to Overdrive (a library program). Kobo also has a cool map feature where you can see where your readers are located throughout the world.

Apple Books

https://authors.apple.com/

Oh yes, Apple is in the self-publishing game, too! You truly learn something new every day, don't you? Apple Books for Authors has writing tools (which may also help you with format-ting), plus they have author interviews, publishing tools, and other resources. You can also put your audiobooks on there (if you happen to have your book in audiobook form). If you're a die-hard Apple person, this might be your go-to place to learn about alter-native publishing!

Aggregate Publishers

If you are just in no mood after finishing that whole Amazon upload and would prefer to just use an aggregate publisher for these top alternate sites as well as all of the other more obscure marketplaces (and there are *hundreds* of them), as well as libraries, I totally feel that. So let's talk about the various aggregate services. (An aggregate publisher is a service that takes your book and distributes it to their list of libraries and partners.)

Just so you know, here are some factoids about aggregate publishers in general:

—Most of them have ebook conversion tools (not necessarily formatting)

—They take your book and distribute it to retailers and bookstores (all different ones, some of which overlap)

—They have collective measurement and royalty features, meaning they will tell you how much you made on each platform

— Each will give you their best marketing insights

— They each have different partnerships with different retailers, meaning there is no one aggregator to rule them all, so you'll need to mix and match if you truly want your book to be (virtually) everywhere.

Personally, I use PublishDrive and StreetLib to distribute my ebooks, and I have been really happy with both of them, but you can choose any one of these (with costs ranging from ones that are free but take a commission, to straight-up paid services that don't). I would recommend taking a look at each one and maybe signing up for a free account on them to see which one appeals to you. Depending on what you need distribution-wise and what you prefer in terms of ease of use on a website, eventually, you will build a set of services and tools that work for you.

Here is a list of the most popular aggregate publishers, along with a few highlights of each. This list is evolving as I get more information (yay for self-publishing!). You're free to sign up for one or all of them—the only thing you'll need to keep track of is who is distributing what and where, so that there are no overlaps. You just need to read the terms for each site carefully and only have each service distribute to places you don't have covered elsewhere.

Draft2Digital

www.draft2digital.com

Draft2Digital has a full-on formatting software suite (not just conversion, if you'll recall my numerous rants about ebook formatting), plus they have a different set of distribution partners. They actually just bought Smashwords, the oldest of the OG book aggregators, which is good news for everyone who uses either of those services.

Here's a YouTube video where both of the CEOs are interviewed about the acquisition, if this is the kind of thing that interests you: https://loriculwell.com/smash

PublishDrive

www.publishdrive.com

PublishDrive is a streamlined service that is mostly subscription based, meaning they have stopped doing the model where they offer a free account with royalty share. This is good for authors who sell a lot of books because once you surpass the flat fee, you're getting a great deal. They have a conversion app and marketing insights, plus they're adding new features all the time.

. . .

One cool and unique thing about PublishDrive is that they have a deal with Amazon that allows you to run paid Amazon advertising on books even if those books are not self-published. If you happen to be in a traditionally or hybrid published situation, this is a super handy feature.

StreetLib
www.streetlib.com

StreetLib has the full suite of features, plus they distribute to Latin America if that's important to you. They also have more of a presence in Africa, so if you're from there, or your books focus on those areas, they might be a better fit for you. They also distribute podcasts.

IngramSpark
www.ingramspark.com

I'm mentioning IngramSpark last, not because they deserve to be last, but because there is overlap here between the world of ebooks and print books, and because I truly think IngramSpark is the best bang for your buck in terms of combined distribution. If you are going to pay their $49 setup fee to distribute your print book, go ahead and just take them up on their combo offer to also distribute your ebook, since they have global distribution and 40,000 retailers.

For print books, the industry best practice is to take your book over to IngramSpark, pay their setup fee (which, as of this book's publication, is $49), and let them do your book's "expanded distribution" instead of checking the "expanded distribution" box at the end of the print publication process (which I covered in Chapter 13).

Note: you will not be able to re-use Amazon's free ISBN on IngramSpark's platform, so you will either need to get a free one from them, or go over to Bowker and buy one. If you're finding this "multiple free ISBNs" situation aggravating already, definitely buy a block of ISBNs for your next book.

See how optimistic I am that you're going to put out a "next book"?

Okay. I've given you a lot of new things to think about here, so with that, I will tell you one last thing, then leave you to go forth and distribute throughout the world!

That one last thing is a caveat: please be clear that when I am telling you about aggregate publishers, I am referring to them only as distribution channels. In no way am I implying that you should buy a done-for-you publishing package with any of these places. I didn't say that! Don't say I said that! You're almost done with this book, which means you do not need to give your money (and power) away to a done-for-you service.

17
MY POST-LAUNCH LIST (OR, A WHOLE BUNCH OF THINGS TO DO ONCE YOUR BOOK IS PUBLISHED)

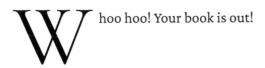 hoo hoo! Your book is out!

I'm not going to stop saying that. I am super excited for you!

Here is my post-launch punch list for some things I think you should do once your book is available. These are in a particular order because each one builds on the other. Do not sleep on this list! The first weeks after your book goes live are arguably the most important, as those weeks are your book's "honeymoon period" in Amazon. The "honeymoon period" is when Amazon is pushing your book up to the top of its algorithm to see if people are liking it (I am not making this up—I have verified this with my own books and the books of clients). If you make the effort to get some sales during this same period, they will keep showing the book (as well as ranking you for more keywords and key phrases). True story!

Now that your book is done, the marketing portion of the program has just begun!

I hope I made this clear enough in chapter 7 when we had that marketing talk: Your book is not going to sell itself. Just having it out there is a huge accomplishment and you should be totally proud, but if you are also going to expect people to actually buy it, you'll need to put some work into that part. Makes sense, right? Also, doing the things on this list will keep you from falling into the "author trap," where you sit around, check your sales reports (or sales rank) a million times a day, then fall into a depression because you think no one wants to buy your book. That is not true! Think about it this way: people would want to buy your books if they knew about you and your books! It is your job to find those people!

So, here are the things you should absolutely do once your book is live:

1. **Order author copies.** One thing you'll definitely need to do once your book is live is to order author copies, like, right away, because they take a while to arrive. Unlike the proof copy you ordered at the end of the publishing process, author copies will be re-sellable, which you can do at book signings and appearances once you have those lined up. There are two ways to order author copies—and (of course) the cheaper one takes longer, so I'll start there.

This first method is for when you need 10 copies or more and you have a long lead time to wait for your books (like, two weeks or longer). Log back into KDP, find your book, and click this button:

Order author copies

Pretty straightforward so far. Great!

Next you'll see this interface:

ORDER QUANTITY

¡ You can order up to 999 copies at a time. Having issues entering the quantity you want?

MARKETPLACE OF YOUR ORDER

Please select a marketp... ∨

This is another one of those "gotcha" moments I'm fond of warning you about. It's not explained very well in the interface, so I'm going to tell you what to do: Amazon is asking you how many author copies of your book you want to buy, and they are going to give you a screaming deal on those copies, basically only charging you what it costs them to print the book.

Because they're Amazon, though, they are going to make up the difference somewhere, and in this scenario, that place is in the shipping. If you make the mistake of ordering one author copy, the shipping cost will make that one copy astronomically expensive, so do yourself a favor and only place this kind of order when you need 10 copies or more.

. . .

Here's yet another gotcha moment—and if you have read this far, this is also one of those "this book just paid for itself" moments.

Once you get to the checkout part of the order, you'll notice that, in fact, Amazon is trying to pull another fast one and trick you into spending some more money by defaulting over to the "two day shipping" option. That looks like this:

Choose a delivery option:
○ **1 business day once shipped**
   $37.99 - One-Day Shipping
◉ **Tuesday, Feb. 8**
   $19.99 - Two-Day Shipping
○ **3-5 business days once shipped**
   $8.00 - Standard Shipping

Oh, snap (or whatever the kids are saying now). Did you see that? Amazon is counting on the fact that you never even double-check the shipping options in your real life because they know you probably order everything with Prime, where shipping is free. If you do not catch this, you will end up dramatically overpaying for your author copies, and you'll be rightfully pissed! And just to add insult to injury, that two-day shipping you'd be overpaying for doesn't even kick in until the books are shipped.

. . .

That right there is a stupid huge waste of money! Keep your eyes peeled for that moment, and this book will have paid for itself two or three times over, my friends.

Lastly, probably because they are being sold at cost, author copies are placed at the very back of the printing queue, so it'll take about two weeks for your box of books to get to you. Also, because Amazon is doing you a favor by selling you these at cost, they are not going to apologize (like, at all) or help you if your books are delayed. They will start out by telling you the books will "usually ship in 10 days," but if something goes wrong, you'll just have to wait.

Wow. I clearly have a lot of feelings about this whole process. Can you tell I've learned some of these lessons the hard way? I actually re-confirmed this just recently while trying to explain this process to a new author in a self-publishing Facebook group. She was absolutely dismayed to learn all of this information too late and ended up going to her book signing empty-handed because her author copies didn't arrive.

The other way to get author copies is to lower the price of your book so that you're barely making any profit (in your KDP dashboard), wait for that change to go through, and then use your regular account to order copies of the book through Prime. Some authors prefer to order all of their copies this way because it's faster and you don't have to run the weird shopping cart gauntlet I described above, but you still end up paying more for your book, so that's reason enough (for me at least) to not make that kind of thing a regular practice.

· · ·

So, do one or more of these things to get some books coming your way because you'll need them to sell, to send out for reviews, and to give away to your friends and family!

2. Make a 3D mockup of your book cover. If you took me up on my free ebook offer from Chapter 7, you are already familiar with the 3D mockup. If not, take your book's Kindle/ebook cover over to https://diybookcovers.com/3Dmockups/, make a 3D version of your book cover, download it, and save it in your "Design" folder for the future. Here's a fancy example!

3. Get some reviews. This is when having an email list of super fans and advance readers would really come in handy. If you have that, definitely email that list as soon as the book is live to let them know you would love some reviews. Note: On your next time through the self-publishing process (which you will find infinitely easier, I promise!), you'll want to send out your manuscript to readers as soon as it is finalized so that they can be ready to write you some good reviews during your launch week. Next time around, make yourself a launch calendar that coincides with the development and production of the book and remind yourself to send ARCs (advanced reader copies) out to reviewers at the one-month out mark. You'll get there!

If you don't have this list yet and are just going to rely on friends and family, that's fine, but tread carefully. I will warn you up front that your friends and family reviews and ratings may not stick. Amazon is always tracking patterns, and if they start seeing the same person leaving reviews on all of your books, they will put it together if that person, say, has the same name as you or mentions that they would like this book even if they weren't, say, your mom. Once they figure this out, they will remove all of the reviews that person (or persons) has written. What I'm saying is this: try to be as subtle as possible when using friends and family for reviews.

In case you think reviews are not important, please let me remind you that Amazon itself says that "91% of shoppers read reviews." Here's a little blurb from them, discussing just how important reviews are:

To summarize: **They** are saying that reviews are super important, and you need them for social proof (to get strangers to buy your book); *I* am saying you need reviews and ratings for Amazon's internal SEO linking process.

· · ·

4. **Work on your Amazon Author Central page.** If you've published anything previously (even with a traditional publisher), you'll already have an Amazon Author Central page in Amazon's system, and you can find that at https://author.amazon.com. If you're a brand-new author, check that link early and often. Your page is either being made or is brand-new and just waiting for you. What you probably did not know is that Amazon actually gives you the opportunity to customize the whole thing. Here are some things you'll probably need to set up:

After you've found your profile at https://author.amazon.com/profile, you'll want to add photos of yourself and your books, your bio, your social media, and a link to the blog feed that comes from your author website. Amazon does pull in the live updates from your blog's feed, so that's also an excellent opportunity for you to get some high-authority backlinks going back over to your website (which will, in turn, build that site's authority in Google). Amazon has also given authors the ability to upload short videos to these pages, which is an amazing opportunity for us to become "real people" and engage readers. As usual, I will advise you that if Amazon gives you some space, fill it up!

When you're done with that, move on to https://author.amazon.com/books, just to make sure your book is listed on there. If it's not, click this button and search for your book by title or ASIN:

Add a Book

You'll then find your book and claim it so it will appear on the page. This is also an excellent opportunity for you to clean up your author page by requesting the removal of any books that you actually didn't write, are out of print, or generally don't belong on your page.

In case you have no idea what I'm talking about, I mean this:

Which, when you click my name, takes you over to my Amazon Author Central page:

This is your chance to put all of your books in one place and tell readers more about yourself as an author, but it does have to be set up properly, so get on that!

• • •

5. Put A+ content modules on your book's listing. This is that moment I was talking about way back in Chapter 6, where I was encouraging you to expand your book's description because you'd need it later. This is also another chance for you to use your 3D mockup of your book cover!

Because your book is self-published, you have the unique opportunity to use A+ content to promote it. A+ for KDP is a rather recent tool available to authors (and author/publishers), having only crossed over from the retail side of Amazon in 2021.

In case you haven't noticed it in action, some book listings now have this kind of thing in their "From the Publisher" section, which looks like this:

Or this:

As you can see, A+ is a much more visually appealing and available way of getting people to learn more about your book, and is way more elegant than the "Look Inside the Book" feature. That feature takes forever to show up after publication, plus Amazon has never been able to get that feature to work on mobile. A+ is much better because it gives you the chance to show and describe the book on the actual listing rather than requiring the customer to do more work to look inside. Fantastic!

To get to the A+ content feature, go to your book in your KDP library and click the "Promote and Advertise" link. That's this guy right here:

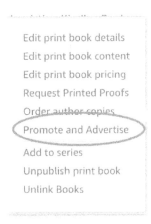

From there, you'll choose the marketplace where you would like to use the A+ Content on your listing (you'll need to repeat this for each marketplace where A+ is offered, but you can repurpose your graphics and information for each one).

You'll then be in the A+ content manager, where you can choose from different A+ modules to build your enhanced content and submit it for review. Here are some good things for you to know, just to wrap up this point:

—Be sure to review the content guidelines (which you can find here https://kdp.amazon.com/en_US/help/topic/G4WB7VPPEARE HAAD) before you build your A+ content and submit it for review. This is a new feature (for publishers), so Amazon has all of the content on manual review, and they will reject anything that looks even remotely spammy to them. Some things you cannot put in your A+ content include (but are by no means limited to): editorial reviews (use your Author Central page for those), pricing details, promotional details (like "free bonus"), or calls to action (like "Buy Now"). Basically, A+ is just there to tell people more about the book and show them graphics of the inside to entice them to buy it without having to "Look Inside."

— There are 17 different choices for A+ modules. Pick the three that best reflect what you're trying to do with your book.

— For some of the modules, you'll need to use a graphic design program (I like Canva) to build the graphics. Amazon provides you with the exact dimensions for the images, so just plug those in and create something that showcases the features of your book.

— Once you're done adding content, you'll need to apply the ASIN (you can find your book's ASIN on your Amazon listing). Click "Apply Content," then click "Review and Submit." This process is still a little clunky and requires one more step than you would think, so make sure you actually submitted it before you leave the A+ interface. You will hear back as to whether they have accepted your A+ content.

Obviously, with 17 modules and an infinite number of combinations for each listing, there is no "one size fits all" approach to A+ content, so you'll need to go in there and determine which modules would be useful for what you're trying to do with your book. Don't leave it blank, though!

. . .

6. Get your reporting in place. I am a big believer that authors should be keeping a very close eye on their sales, so they can know what's working and replicate it (or change up their strategies if things aren't working). For this reason, I use several reporting tools (that I look at multiple times per day), and I suggest you do the same. Reporting is where the rubber meets the road in terms of thinking of yourself as a business person (not just a creative person), so you'll only want to really keep track of your reporting if it's something you care about. Obviously, do not do any of this marketing and measurement stuff if you just want to see your book in print! You don't care about these numbers!

The first place you can go to see your results is the "Reports" tab in KDP. I don't really care for how the data is laid out in the initial screen (mostly because it doesn't tell you which books have sold), so I would recommend clicking the blue link labeled "Try the new KDP Reports beta," rather than trying to make sense of the weird bar graphs and charts.

When you click that link, you'll immediately see how much you've made that day in royalties, plus it'll break those sales down by top-selling books. There are also several other features in there, like a Royalties Estimator and a sort function that will let you go back and see your historic sales by book. Those are useful (and again, much better than nothing!), and I would definitely recommend going in there and playing around with the functionality.

There are some limitations to the KDP Reports Beta (by the way, this feature has been in beta for several years, and I haven't noticed them adding anything to it, but I'm not behind the scenes, so what do I know?). For one, you can only pull reports going back three years, which is not super helpful to those of us who have been publishing for a long time. They will also not let you know when you sell a book, which means you'll need to go back in there multiple times a day to see if anything is happening.

Also, file this under "good to know": printed books appear in your royalties *the day they are shipped*, not the day people buy them. Kindle books are delivered electronically, so those royalties usually appear the same day. Keep this in mind when you hear from people that they bought your book, but you haven't yet seen the sales show up. Don't worry—they're coming!

Overall, KDP Reports might be enough for you, especially if you're self-publishing for the first time and are just trying to keep your head above water with all of this new information. If you've taken a look at the KDP reporting functionality and (like myself) have found it to be rather lacking, I would highly recommend checking out KDP Champ (https://kdpchamp.com), which is a third-party reporting software that I use. I have tried all of the other reporting websites out there, and I can honestly say that KDP Champ is head and shoulders above the others. They will even send you an email every time you make a sale!

One of the things I love most about this particular reporting software is that they don't actually have access to your data. I usually recommend against giving third-party software or websites of any kind access to your sales information, because those data are basically your trade secrets, and I object on principle to the concept of giving developers an open invitation to all of your back-end data. KDP Champ doesn't do that.

Once you are used to finding and reacting to your Amazon sales, log in to all of the "alternate" distribution channels you signed up for in the last chapter and make sure you know where to look for sales there. You will need to put yourself on a schedule for looking at those (I do it on the 1st and 15th of every month).

7. **Run some paid advertising to your book on Amazon.** Let me state upfront that I am not advising you to pay for any advertising unless and until you have that all-important link inside your book to the landing page with the incentivized signup on it. Without the means to convert the reader to a subscriber in place, you are essentially just running money through Amazon to make one-time sales of books rather than building your career. I hope you are hearing me on this.

Here are the basic steps for running an automatically targeted ad —and I am going to speed through this because this book is already pretty long and I know you're exhausted (I certainly am). Go over to advertising.Amazon.com and set up your account. They will need you to enter a credit card to pay for your ad spend in advance even though they are going to pay you 60 days in arrears (meaning if you sell a book today, you receive your royalties two months from now). Such is life on Amazon!

What you'll want to do is take out three different ads for your book: Automatic Targeting, Category, and Manual. I'm covering

"General" here so this chapter doesn't turn into another one of those monster tomes.

For Automatic (or "auto) ads, you're basically just giving Amazon permission to show your book when people search for what it deems to be similar titles. You're kind of taking your chances on this one because you don't know exactly what Amazon thinks your book is about yet, but if you followed all the steps in the keyword and category research chapters, you should be fine.

Here are the standard settings for an automatic targeting ad:

—Daily budget: $5.00 (you're probably not going to spend this, but log in and keep an eye on it if the concept makes you nervous.)

—Campaign-bidding strategy: Dynamic bids, down only

—Ad format: Standard

The auto-targeting setting is especially important. Amazon is always going to set the default bid to something crazy like $.75 or $1.00 per click, which you should not agree to, even if your book is selling great and you make $5 in royalty per copy. This is just their opening offer! Never take the opening offer! For real, change that bid to something like $.10 per click.

· · ·

You'll then start two more new ads: a manual keywords ad where you'll use the keywords you found in chapter 4, and a categories ad, where you use the categories you found in chapter 6. Even more repurposing of previous work! Amazing!

8. Get your book indexed and ranked by Google. I am an SEO nerd by profession, so eventually it was going to come to this. Bear with me. When you publish your book on Amazon, you are wanting Amazon's algorithm to see it and pick it up so it appears in searches and ranks for keywords and key phrases within Amazon itself. What I'm talking about here is actually the macrocosm of that, where you get Google to index your book's listing on Amazon, so you and your book appear in Google searches, like so (these are the Google search results for my website book):

This is important because Google is still the #1 search engine in the world, and when your book appears in its search results, that's going to cause external traffic (and potential customers) to flow into Amazon, which in turn will trigger Amazon's algorithm to show your book to its own internal customers even more. It's a true symbiosis. Google considers Amazon to be an ultimate "authority site," which means that anytime you search for something in Google that you need to buy, you will find an Amazon listing on page one for that phrase. Despite these two playing so well together, there is no straightforward way to get Amazon listings to "jump" into Google searches, so most authors will just publish their books and hope that eventually Google eventually takes notice.

Because you have taken all of my advice and did proper keyword in the prep section, then used those keywords in everything from your book's subtitle to its description, you have created a perfectly optimized listing for Google to fall in love with.

If you are still awake, boy are you lucky, because I have a free bonus for you! I want to help you get your book out there, so I'm offering a free bonus to anyone who gets to the end of this guide, publishes their book, and reaches out to me.

You might not have totally understood the inner workings of my whole spiel about Amazon SEO, but just to show my appreciation to you for buying this book—and my admiration for you for actually finishing your book and getting it out there—I would be happy to put your book's listing through my own software that I personally use to get Google to index book listings.

· · ·

To get this bonus, all you have to do is go over and fill out this form: https://loriculwell.com/booklinks

That was a lot, and really, that's about it for the list of things you can do for your book if you don't have an author platform yet. If you do have one set up, let's move on to the next chapter!

18

ADVANCED BOOK MARKETING

Okay, we're almost done!

Say, remember that (really harsh) "Marketing Bare Minimum" talk we had way back in chapter 7 when we barely knew each other? Since then, we've been in the self-publishing trenches together, something I hope you will keep in mind as I make my way down this marketing-intensive list.

Because, friends, this chapter presupposes a number of things: that you have chosen the "indie author/ publisher" path in that cross-roads in your mind, that you have put together an author website, an email list, and social media that is author-specific (or at least where people know you're an author and expect you to mention a book every once in awhile), and that you are mentally prepared to start really putting yourself out there in a big way.

. . .

To close this book out strong, here's a list of more advanced marketing tips to send you on your way with your newly-published book in hand.

1. Post your book, and links to all the places to buy it, on your author website. I know I don't need to make the point yet again (and certainly not in all caps) that I once again STRONGLY recommend you build your author website. It's the hub for everything in your author life, and you'll need it to build up your audience. Plus, now you have something to put on it!

You can put your books and their links on your website in a few different ways: You can use a plugin like Books Gallery or Book-Press, you can manually add all the links to the site, or you can use a tool like https://books2read.com/, which was literally created just for this exact purpose. Plus, the good news is, if your author website has an RSS feed function and you've added that to your Amazon Author Central page, your updates will appear there as well!

You'll also want to grab the 3D mockup of the ebook cover you have saved in the folder for your designs and put it somewhere prominent on the website. Be sure to include the links for all of the places where people can buy your book, including Amazon, Barnes & Noble, Apple iBooks, and wherever else you put your book in Chapter 17.

. . .

2. Send an announcement about your book to your email list. If you have an email list, now is the absolute perfect moment to send an email to the people on that list announcing your book launch. Your list has people on it who signed up because they like you and they want to hear more about what you're doing, to celebrate your victories with you, and to cheer you on!

So take that 3D mockup of your book cover (yes, again) and use it as the focal point for a newsletter that's totally dedicated to your book's launch.

3. Post an announcement about your book (with a link!) on all of your social media platforms. Ideally, you will have multiple social media channels as part of your author platform, and will have a launch strategy that includes mentions of your book, so now's the time to get the word out!

Don't do this in an obnoxious way and make sure not to repeat yourself too much (or you'll risk annoying your friends and violating the terms of service of most social media platforms), but definitely let your friends and family know about your big achievement. And definitely use that 3D mockup book cover when you post!

And be sure to post to *all* of your social media—Twitter, LinkedIn, your Facebook profile, your Facebook Author Page, Pinterest, Instagram, and so on. Talk about it on your YouTube channel if you have one, make TikToks about your book (or about yourself), basically do more of whatever you do! For social media platforms that don't allow direct linking, make sure you include photos and mentions of your book (yet another reason to order those author copies!).

4. Start really ramping up your participation on your social media outlet of choice. Answer questions on Reddit, LinkedIn, or in Facebook groups. Make TikToks, post up more photos on Instagram, post YouTube videos, or whatever you do the most. Just make sure that every one of your profiles has a clear path back to that all-important author website, which should now have a whole page dedicated just to your new book, as well as a way to sign up for your email list. (It's official, I am never going to shut up about that list.)

For real, though, whatever you do for social media, you should start doing it much more now. Not for the purpose of shouting "I wrote a book!" into the proverbial void, but just to raise your overall profile as a person, and to get traffic going over to your website, and, by extension, your book. Now's the time to get yourself out there!

5. Put your ebook on "permafree." As I mentioned briefly way back when we were discussing KDP Select, some authors choose a strategy called "permafree" as a way to get readers into their work and to build up their email lists. "Permafree" is when your book is always free on all marketplaces. Amazon obviously doesn't really want you doing this, so the only way to achieve the "zero" price tag is through a sneaky workaround I will describe here.

Now, before you do this, definitely make sure you have a strong lead magnet on your author website (meaning you are giving something away for free to entice people to sign up for your email list) and that the website and the incentive are both mentioned in the front and back of your book (with an active link, of course). Also, make sure that any other books in the series are clearly linked at the back of your book. If you are going to give something away for free, you want to get something (new readers) in return!

To execute the "permafree" strategy, just go over to one of the aggregators you're using to distribute your book more widely. Change your book's price to "free," then wait for that change to populate across the platforms to which that aggregator distributes. You just need ONE of Amazon's competitors (like Barnes & Noble or Apple iBooks) to start showing your book as free, then you can make your next move.

Once your book is free on another "major" marketplace, grab the link to that listing, log in to your KDP dashboard, and send an email to KDP Support (exactly how you did it when you asked Amazon to add your book to additional categories in Chapter 16), and request that they price match the other marketplace and set your book's price to zero.

Yes, it sounds crazy, but that's the only way to do it! If you happen to get a customer service rep that doesn't know about this policy and rejects your request, try again in a few days.

That's it! Go forth and tell the world about your book. You've worked super hard, and you deserve the recognition and accolades that come with being a published author!

· · ·

If you're super into learning about book marketing (or have just realized that you need to get interested), I'm happy to offer you a free workbook that walks you through everything I cover in my book "How to Market a Book." You can find that over at: https://loriculwell.com/htmabguide .

19
YOU MADE IT!

Well, here we are! You've reached the end of this book, and hopefully *you* now have a book of your own. Allow me to say just how proud I am of you for hanging in there throughout this whole process. It wasn't easy, and you did it!

Feel free to let me know if you found anything confusing, if you think I should go into more detail on any concept (Ha! What are the chances someone is going to say that?), or even if you had a weird experience with Amazon that you think I might find interesting or have some insight on. I've heard everything at least once, so I'm sure I'll be able to help.

I'll close by saying that if this book has just changed your life and you are now a bestselling author, or even if this book just enriched you in some way, I'm so grateful. And if you'd like to reach out to say a nice thing or leave a review, that would be grand!

. . .

I wish you the best of luck on your self-publishing journey. Congratulations!

WHAT ELSE CAN I TEACH YOU?

If you have enjoyed our time together so much that you would like to read some other stuff I've written, here are some other books in the "Funny You Should Ask" series!

How to Make a Website: the 100% Not-Boring Guide to Setting Up Your Website with Wordpress

How to Do Search Engine Optimization: SEO for Marketing, Blogging, and More

How to Market a Book: The Hilariously Detailed Guide to Author Marketing and Book Promotion

How to Sell More Books: The Missing Piece of Your Author Marketing Strategy

How to Publish Low Content Books: Publishing Journals, Notebooks, and More on KDP

Milton Keynes UK
Ingram Content Group UK Ltd.
UKHW022320020424
440481UK00015B/686

9 798869 015518